Where
the
Rivers
Join

Where the Rivers Join

A personal account of healing from ritual abuse

Beckylane

Press Gang Publishers
Vancouver

The Publisher gratefully acknowledges financial assistance from the Canada Council, the Book Publishing Industry Development Program of the Department of Canadian Heritage, and the Cultural Services Branch, Province of British Columbia.

CANADIAN CATALOGUING IN PUBLICATION DATA

Beckylane.
 Where the rivers join

 ISBN 0-88974-043-7

 1. Adult child abuse victims—Biography. 2. Ritual abuse victims—Biography. 3. Ritual abuse. 4. Healing. I. Title.
HV6626.5.B42   1995   362.7´64´092   C95-910129-2

Author's note: For reasons of emphasis, ellipses have not been inserted in quotations which begin or end mid-sentence. All sources are cited in the bibliography.

My heartfelt thanks to the women at press gang / for your sensitivity to word and image / for your gentleness of spirit / for your courage

Edited by Barbara Kuhne
Design and cover photography by Val Speidel
Typeset in Fournier
Printed on acid-free paper by Best Book Manufacturers
Printed and bound in Canada

Press Gang Publishers
101 - 225 East 17th Avenue
Vancouver, B.C.   V5V 1A6
Canada

To those of you
who've suffered and/or died
and who still suffer and/or die
at the hands of ritual abuse
slaughterers

The hard work of a non-racist sensibility is the boundary crossing, from safe circle to wilderness: the testing of boundary, the consecration of sacrilege. It is the willingness to spoil a good party and break an encompassing circle, to travel from the safe to the unsafe. The transgression is dizzyingly intense, a reminder of what it is to be alive. It is a sinful pleasure, this willing transgression of a line, which takes one into new awareness, a secret, lonely, and tabooed world — to survive the transgression is terrifying and addictive. To know that everything has changed and yet that nothing has changed; and in leaping the chasm of this impossible division of self, a discovery of the self surviving, still well, still strong, and, as a curious consequence, renewed.

— Patricia Williams

I think that the hard work of a ritual abuse survivor who actively and repeatedly breaks the silence is like

LETTER TO BECKYLANE:
RE: DEFAMATION AGAINST OUR CLIENT

We are acting as counsel for _____ .

We are advised that you have made serious allegations against him. Our instructions are that such statements are false and designed only to harm our client's reputation. As such they constitute defamation.

Because you have sent copies of your statement to members of our client's family, there has been publication of the defamation.

Although there is a clear case against you, our client will not involve you in litigation, provided you immediately cease the sending of such letters.

In the event that further letters are sent, our client may have no other choice but to proceed with a lawsuit against you.

Defamation.   Holding up of a person to ridicule, scorn or contempt in a respectable and considerable part of the community; may be criminal as well as civil. Includes both libel and slander.

Defamation is that which tends to injure reputation; to diminish the esteem, respect, goodwill or confidence in which the plaintiff is held, or to excite adverse, derogatory or unpleasant feelings or opinions against [that person]. Statement which exposes person to contempt, hatred, ridicule or obloquy. McGowen v. Prentice, La.App., 341 So.2d 55, 57. The unpriviledged publication of false statements which naturally and proximately result in injury to another. Wolfson v. Kirk, Fla.App., 273 So.2d 774, 776.

A communication is defamatory if it tends so to harm the reputation of another as to lower [that person] in the estimation of the community or to deter third persons from associating or dealing with [that person]. The meaning of a communication is that which the recipient correctly, or mistakenly but reasonably, understands that it was intended to express. Restatement, Second, Torts §§559, 563.

— *Black's Law Dictionary*, 5th Edition

FOREWORD

Where the Rivers Join is about memory, trauma and a woman's unconquerable spirit. It is a poetic trail, a triumphant journey, beset with huge obstacles, requiring the sort of heroism we should never be called upon to exhibit. This journey is full of wonder; it begs the reader to sit quiet and follow it through in one graceful movement. Nothing is requested of us but to listen.

Indigenous belief holds that each child is a creative being, possessing her own spirit, sense of justice and emotional self. If her life experiences nurture her individual spirit and emotional being, the sense of justice she is born with blossoms and her innate creativity is actualized. If she lives in a state of trauma, her life memories will contradict the sense of justice which is her birthright. Where memory and spiritual justice collide, our responses to past, present and future become tangled. Memory, which provides us with a basis for ordering up the chaos of our lives, establishing a sense of what is normal and what we can expect in the future, can no longer serve as a guide to the future. When this occurs the internal conflict may force the individual to abandon memory.

Memory is emotional, spiritual, intellectual and physical. The spirit of each child is capable of knowing which memories a child can assimilate and process and which experiences are not understandable. When an experience is too painful for a child to understand, the spirit and the body of the child move to hide the memory, blocking its resurfacing until the child is able to come to grips with the pain, the horror and the injustice. In many cases of severe trauma the memories may remain locked/frozen until the child becomes an adult. Should the child be forced to remember too soon, suicide often results.

Traumatic memories do not return full blown. They generally return in snippets, images, pieces which initially make little or no sense to the adult. Nightmarish pictures collide with current reality, creating confusion for the individual. The distance created by physically locking memories away, hiding them in the child's body, far from her spirit, creates disbelief in the adult. Personal doubt is compounded by a sense of alienation from the middle-class images of respectability and idyllic family life. Believing that only their life did not reflect the ideal, many survivors remain silent. Beckylane broke the web of silence when her hand met the courage of her spirit within, found a pen and committed her first unlocked memory to the page. Image by image, snippet by snippet, the "big ugly" unfolds in the pages of Beckylane's journal. As the unravelling of the memories occurs she reclaims her life, reclaims her personal self and struggles with disbelief, doubt, horror and bondage. We read and follow the trail just as it happened.

Those readers who have hidden memories may find them triggered by this work. Your own blocked memories may surface. Seek help if reading this book brings on nightmares. Those of you who have bought the image of the ideal family and middle-class respectability may have trouble with your belief systems. Some may find the horror too shocking to believe. I have witnessed the unraveling of memory in adult Native people who lived in trauma as children attending residential schools. For them and countless other people raised in deviant states of "normalcy," this eloquent account is all too familiar. I hope that the work before you leads to the sort of gentle loving indignation that it calls up in myself. The lives of women and children are taken much too lightly in this maddened patriarchal world.

I am moved to wonder at the amazing things this spirited and heroic woman could have accomplished had she not been forced upon this path. I am heartened that she was able to track her journey and resist the victimization of her adult self. The survivor who is still struggling to recover from the experiences described in the following pages is a remarkable woman.

Lee Maracle
Brampton, Ontario

Where
the
Rivers
Join

I am a poet. what follows is an act of self-love,
not-a-poem and hence not-a-poetic-license,
not-a-deviation from fact, form or rule by
an artist or writer for the sake of the
effect gained:

large bed no sheets old musty mattress
    nothing else in the room hardwood floor my daddy
carries me scared daytime scared in
    that room it's okay honey I'll protect you your
guardian angel's here daddy loves you

A DREAM: I'm inside a cold damp clinical building. a person
stands beside an operating table white robe face blood
streams down. blank smile knowing not unfriendly silent.
the person is me.
off in another room, a dismembered man is being repaired
without anaesthetic. women come to look at him a spectacle
they're curious to see a mutilated man blood and bones pain.
he yells at them an old man's voice hoarse from smoking or
singing both maybe. he's spirited and lively disdainful
barks at each woman when she walks in. barks until the next.
"come in here to watch did ya? had to see all this blood and
guts and gore. thrill-seeker, eh? you should be ashamed
getting your kicks this way."
none of them know him. none of them love him.
I want to go in but I'm afraid of the power in his voice.
the hate. I've seen him suffer and I've seen his pain but he
was unconscious at the time and he wouldn't remember he
would think I was one of the others. I helped him and I
became attached to him but he wouldn't know that. he'd yell
at me like at the others and I'd remain silent during his
tirade because my fear would block my self.

mar 20 / 91
almost a month. finally I can look at the dream.
it's his blood the old man's my dad's blood that streams the front
of my face in the dream. running down into the ground. cold.
why do I feel shame? she doesn't. she feels no shame the she
that's me in the dream. I don't see her until the end. she knows
something. why do I feel fear? she doesn't. she is content. she
wears a white frock. she's a healer. I am a healer.
why is dismemberment "help"?
his blood is coming out of me, my head.

may 13 / 91
I want to separate from my daddy. I want him out of me.

(1) Some agency is doing something terrible to you; (2) you have
no idea how long it will last; and (3) you have no control over it.
These are the elements of extreme trauma.

Does the child report being defecated and urinated upon; report
having to ingest both?

Does the child describe the torture and killing of animals
(may include drinking their blood)?

may 22 / 91
group sex.
my dad pours warm milk fresh cow milk goat milk sometimes all
over me all over me bare naked and then gets animals to lick it
off. dog. cow. sheep. pig. pig's his favourite.
my dad fucks the animal sometimes. pig's his favourite.
I still can't eat pork broth. can't be on a pig farm.
humiliated. sometimes my dad and his friends would laugh and
laugh. some with white teeth. some yellow. brown. some no
teeth. teeth missing. titillated, all of them.
group sex too. my dad carries me to a room all nice and warm he
says I love you my little angel daddy's girl.

Your wisdom has kept you
far away from dangers.

may 23 / 91
the incested wounded me is quiet unable to speak choked
silenced humiliated. humiliated. humiliated before anyone
everyone even me the woman me. unable to believe the visual
unable to believe wanting to believe wanting to be able to
speak freely. what if that humiliated frightened child whose
tongue's been chopped sliced out were to speak. freely. openly.
what would she say?
help. she would ask for help. daddy doesn't help. mommy
doesn't help.
   what kind of help?
    real
        what's real?
      safe
           what's safe?
          quiet
              what's quiet?
               hug love love real
                         trust?
                              ?

The current year will bring you much happiness.

SAMANTHA: Ah, Mom, maybe we should drive back home. Look. All the kids are wearing shorts and I have pants on today. Do you think it's okay? Do you think I should go home and change?

ME: Well, we can if you want, Samantha. But I think you look pretty good. It's okay to just be yourself, honey. There'll be other kids with pants.

SAMANTHA: How can I just be myself, Mom? I don't even know who I am, so how can I possibly just be myself?

STEPHANIE: You shouldn't make your reader work so hard. You should say that you're going to include fortune cookies in the body of your text. The irony of

Soon you will be sitting on top
of the world.

MARGARET: Your father is responsible. He was the adult.

jun 02 / 91
the surface the church the cleanliness the secrets the impossibility
of fitting reality into some kind of order or even sense

                                        his blood
          cold
              out
                      gone
                                  go away   daddy
              go away
              he masturbated himself with
my arm my hand held there
    my body pinned down
       my arm wretched wrenched bending back behind
       my back him on me heavy penis hot hard on
       my bum
          my arm forced back

jun 03 / 91

I'm so confused. I know if I saw my dad right now, I'd go to his
open arms. I'd try to stop his tears. I would agree with his daft
logic, his sophistry. I'd try to create his world the way he wants it
to go, even though I disappear. silence. a force of silence.

jun 04 / 91

sometimes he was so kind and understanding. warm. sometimes
he made love with such tenderness and affection. he wouldn't let
the men hurt me like they hurt some of the others. children's
naked bodies. some so badly bruised. mine too sometimes.
rubbing blood on me. slippery and him so hot with lust.
it's all so hard to believe. the more I write, the more I'm able to
believe.
at home it seemed okay. violence and loving sexual abuse. loving
abuse. a double, what does it mean? I wanted my dad to do sex
acts with me. I enjoyed it. I wanted it. my dad convinced me,
easily, that it wasn't bad. I believed him because I knew what
was bad. what happened on that farm was bad.

Your cares will lessen if they
are faced cheerfully.

Does the child report being locked inside a cage or "jail"?

they are in the barn　　　　the men
we are in the trap　　　　the kids
*　　　　　　　　fence posts　　　barbed wire thick*
thick nowhere to go sit knees to chin rocking scared shaking
leaning on a post cold
kids around me scared too　　　　some crying quiet
my dad comes to get me　　I feel better　　he tells me to
come to the gate lets me through I know it will hurt I know
*　　　　　　　　　　　　　　if I'm a good girl*
*　　　maybe it won't hurt so long*

The fact that ritual abuse happens is an outrage and a betrayal
that impacts all of humanity. It must be flushed out and stopped.

— Shirley Turcotte [b]

jun 17 / 91
wanting to say something before I go to sleep about how I
feel about my house, about being home. I went around tonight
saying, I hate it I hate it. I haven't cooked cleaned done
laundry well for months. maybe since the house dreams. last
year. my inside
inside my house. why am I feeling this way? I'm healing
inside. so why can't I clean my house? why do I dread coming
here? it's my house, after all. it's not my parents' house.
it's mine. so what's going on?

jun 22 / 91
robbed of my inside. inside was never safe. inside the house
I never knew what would happen. I was never safe. inside me
I couldn't trust I wanted to trust but when I showed myself
for real I was so rejected so

You will attract cultured and artistic
people to your home.

jun 24 / 91

adult vocabulary is so inadequate and useless to describe what's
happening to a child. to say that what those kids and I were doing
was sex is ridiculous. yet there's no way to articulate two children
being forced to violate themselves and have themselves violated
by another kid. neither kid wants to. neither has a whole lot of
sense of "other."

jun 27 / 91

I feel so terrible.
how can I fit the kinds of abuse I'm remembering into some
kind of   me
it's so much and it's so broad and it's so utterly
fantastical. I must be making it up
    remember   make up
    re member   cover up
    find   hide
am I finding or am I hiding?
both. I'm hiding from what I've found.

blue dress white socks black shoes

                   they are all around looking

scary red faces laughing some

          my dad puts me in the stall his breath hot

     him shaking   *I'm scared*

       I cry a little   *not allowed to cry*

the men will beat me if I cry if I'm weak if

                   I'm scared

I want to take my dress off it's new it's pretty it will get

        all full of blood

      my dad goes and asks I look down at the

floor   *onetwothreefourfive*

        it's cement it's painted too

     they all say no

             I'm five

BECKYLANE'S REPORT CARD, AGE 5: Beckylane is doing very good work in all subjects. She is making excellent progress. She is honours calibre.

someone gets a pig and there's the pig and it's a girl she's
crying squealing loud they start to laugh to hit to make
some noise boom boom boom beat
                                        I close my eyes
              they're going to hurt the pig   they do
she's bleeding now they throw her in the stall and near me
                                tell me to hug the pig but I shake my head
                          no
I crouch my dad says let her take off the dress and then
she'll hug the pig now won't you my little angel
                                                      numb I shake my head
                                                             yes
I take off the dress slip and panties white I hug the pig
              red   she's scared and blood and warm
and kind of quiet
                                    they watch the show now
      be good little girl now   no
                                                            I won't

10 Reasons Why I Would Falsely Accuse My Parents of Incest
or Ritual Abuse

  1. I needed a new reason to stay in therapy.
  2. I wanted to suddenly start having
     tremendous difficulty in relating to my
     partner, lose all my trust, and alienate
     her/him to the point where we would
     begin fighting constantly and have to
     break up.

                              — Jezanna Rainforest

jul 06 / 91
a shadow that follows leads goes wherever I go. I still
resist belief. if it didn't happen, why do I feel this way? why
do I carry this shadow? it compresses or spreads out big.
the other day at the zoo, I walked into a building smelled pig,
thought, no beckylane, there goes your imagination get with it.
then looked over a fence, a potbellied vietnamese pig asleep.
immediately went back. thought, no, I made it up. thought, no.
I didn't. I was there. I was there. hello pig. I love you pig.
I know how you feel too.
I felt so much connection with the pig when I was small. I was
swollen and hurting sticky hurting everywhere. the pig must
have been dead. I kissed her better felt pity and love. maybe
for me too.

jul 06 / 91

I don't know what I want to feel. I've felt pity and love for my
dad. I've been so debilitated in so many ways. can't write letters
can't clean house play have much fun. it's because of my fucking
dad. fucked me beat me brutalized me tortured me then loved me
with the tenderness of a saint. me a bundle of confusion. me a
very strange woman. hating my strangeness. hating myself. won-
dering how I could think these terrible things about my own dad.
I'd like to hurt him the way he hurt me. I'd like to scare him and
humiliate him and hear him beg me to stop. I can imagine him
begging. but I would never listen. I'd tape him and play it back
to him on huge speakers loud loud when he tried to sleep and
while he slept if he slept. I'd make him know how it feels to be
robbed of self. to have his psyche bashed with a mallet. beg for
forgiveness, asshole. beg. I'll never give it. never.
I was like the pig, my skin torn off sharp knife through the fat
like through the thick bushes branches flying. my skin removed
by him. exposed flesh.
yes I will hate you, you rot. you fuck. I don't care what happened
to you when you were a kid. you were an adult when you loosed
your lunacy onto me. you knew what you were doing. you knew
you were sick sick sick because you cried about it sometimes.
I was afraid of you. I loved you. I thought I could pray for you
and you'd get better. now I hate you. you are a fuck. I wish you
a long and painful death. I don't ever want to see you again.
never. when I send you a letter of confrontation, I'll believe
myself. my memories. my life. nothing you could say could hurt
me any more. I will do it. I will.

jul 17 / 91
standing naked in the cold raining cold blue skin no one really cares. I feel like I really care about other people but maybe I don't maybe everyone is standing shaking from the cold.

                    I close my eyes tight
                    sharp sting a stick
                    they open
those men they hurt the pig some more don't look don't look
they hit me more and kick me some open your eyes you little
cunt   they cut the pig her skin they
peel it off she's still alive they put the skin on me push
me down on my tummy cold floor I'm sick I'm feeling sick now
crawl you piggy crawl
                    I can't I can't get up I'm sick too
heavy they kick me kick me up get up
                              a man lands hard on me
my back it hurts I have to pee   I pee
                              he grabs my hair
my head rubs blood thick warm sticky all in my hair all in
my hair my face my mouth it's in my mouth open your mouth
you little bitch he hurts me too just like my dad my dad at
home I want to go home it hurts it hurts it hurts

in dream, my house is inside me, me inside.

jul 27 / 91
suddenly it occurs to me that I know how to pack a dead baby
neatly into a sack so it can be carried off and no one could tell by
holding it that it's anything more than rotting potatoes.
I want to be sick.
after spending the week cleaning my room for the first time since
remembering about my dad, today I cleaned the basement for the
first time swept it too.
then I had the image

packing a dead baby
blue bloated in with rotting potatoes

        careful   dirty   sick
        small hands   brown   mine   my hands

my hands packing the baby
he made me pack the baby

                   him laughing
                    laughing

It is the voices of survivors remembering and speaking of their experiences that is creating the window for communities and organizations to hear and act on behalf of all children in the name of compassion, healing and love.

— Shirley Turcotte [b]

aug 02 / 91
the memory looming. looming still wanting me wanting to feel

crying crying sick sick crying can't stop can't stop loud
loud can't stop beat her beat her get the cunt to shut her
fucking trap get her the fuck outta here crying crying can't
stop the baby's dead she's cold she's blue she's dead she's
small no no

                                       no
fuckin pack it cunt   you'll be next
we'll chop ya up like piggy little fuck   shut your
trap ya little fuck   pack it like I told ya
               my head hot hurting   can't stop
crying I want my daddy where's my daddy no more no
                       no more
                                   kick kick can't stop
gagging so sore tummy can't stop crying so sore head loud
loud can't stop can't stop can't

aug 15 / 91

I do deserve my love. without punishment. I was a child when I
did those things. in my own little mind I tried to make some kind
of sensible image of my life. until I packed the baby I thought I
was okay. I could make a picture and somewhere deep inside still
know I was okay. but the combination — my mom my dad me —
no longer fit. I could no longer remain whole. I had to fragment,
to break away, literally, from myself. somewhere during that
three- or four-month period when I couldn't talk, my father
promised he would never take me back there. my mother
promised I could go to my aunty's this summer if I started to
talk. that I must never tell anyone what a bad girl I was. that god
would know and I would never go to heaven.

I am seven rhymes with heaven

aug 15 / 91
my father started to fuck me at home more.
lots. then so tender. gentle. crying.

see   see
daddy loves you so much my little angel

    stiff   warm   comfort   warm
me
                                                          cold
            tears feeling for tears
                                          shuts slams stolen
    you cry I can't cry   shut
    you don't mean it
    you don't mean it
    you your hands large dry warm soft and gentle
        pleasure no this is wrong no I'm your daughter
        sexy wet smells lifted high above the right the
        wrong the world is small is yes
                    oh yes
                            breathing sexy yes
                why can't I just say no
                            shut down the body

                                                            no

     why can't I

         I can't cry

       but I can fuck

         I can fuck and fuck and

wet wet flowing wetness all around the smells of body feels
so good large hands cup small buttocks soft and warm so
gentle skin feels acts wants more

    yes more

       I don't deserve to cry

       I am the same as him

       I don't deserve to cry for me

       I can take his cry and make him better but

       I cannot give my

       I want to give my

I tell my counsellor that I feel love for her, making her important to the process so that I wouldn't make myself into an object, which is what I did as a child, really.

aug 16 / 91
I notice I've been talking about myself my body as if we are separate entities. I am my body. my body is me. I do things that are good for my body as though I'm performing some kind of exercise or plan: this is good for my body; this is not. I am my body. when my body speaks to me it's me speaking to me and when I speak to my body it's me speaking to me.

aug 18 / 91
I can write and write and write in my diary and to what end? what means? I've inherited the past. I am a woman. I'm from lower working class. I'm one little speck. why do I see? what do I see? people are wonderful. all born innocent and wanting happiness, naturally. transformed by experience. unable or unwilling to see that because power reaps, it also destroys.
my own vocabulary limits me. my own reality limits me. I'm not anyone because I lack the accoutrements of power.

Power is cautious. It covers itself. It bases itself in another's pain and prevents all recognition that there is "another" by looped circles that endure its own solipsism.

— Elaine Scarry

A fresh step can lead to the path of riches.

It's sweet to be remembered,
but it's often cheaper to be forgotten.

A SCHOLAR: This is fascinating!!!! No words to describe.
By the time I got to page twenty-eight, I wanted to stop reading.
I did stop reading. But then I decided, no. That's what society
expects us to do. Taboos are supposed to remain taboo. So I read
the rest. It made it somehow easier to read the rest, keeping that
in mind.

Fascinate.   *v.* 1598. 1. To affect by witchcraft; to enchant, lay
under a spell — 1657.

2. To cast a spell over by a look (said *esp.* of
serpents); to render unable to move or
resist 1641.

3. *fig.* To attract and hold the attention of
by an irresistible influence 1651.

4. The serpent fascinates its prey, apparently
by the power of its eyes 1845; a wit that
would fascinate sages; the eye of the
ancient mariner fascinated the wedding
guest; hence, *fascinating.*
— *Concise Oxford Dictionary*

Ritual abuse is a brutal form of abuse in which the victim is assaulted at every conceivable level, usually by multiple perpetrators of both sexes, over an extended period of time. The physical abuse is so severe that it often involves torture and killing. The sexual abuse is typically sadistic, painful, and humiliating. The psychological abuse relies upon terrorization of the victim, mind-altering drugs, and mind-control techniques. The spiritual abuse causes victims to feel that they are so worthless

— Catherine Gould

Among the lucky, you are the chosen one.

it's so hard to keep all the fragments together where did they come from why am I so confused why can't I be unconfused smooth warm? I want to love myself. I want to say, beckylane, you brave woman, look how you've survived. but I say, no. it's all lies. why? why would it be lies? what would I have to gain? why would I want it?

A comfortable salary and good position will be yours.

I want myself
like a dream only real
                    womb smells
              sweet and wonderful

aug 19 / 91

today was a big day for me. my childhood is with me now, my memories moved forward in time. I feel a surge of remembering, a connection with my body, a feeling of pure joy

aug 29 / 91

feeling better. from inside somewhere a strength. it's so important, I know, to keep the strength.

aug 30 / 91

so what's going on? something feels so right here yet I feel like I went to bed one night a child, and woke up the following morning fully adolescent. a new and fuller way of perceiving feeling like a stranger to myself.

aug 31 / 91

I feel my past so new to me my past that part of me I carried without consciousness is here now conscious of where the self-hate manifested of where the negative indoctrination

moving

doing what is in my best interest and waiting for the doom that came to me in the past

waiting for the punishment that's sure to manifest out of my
acting out creatively

sep 01 / 91
yet I know there's no doom. I know I'm different. I'm taking
good care of myself. I can continue to allow myself my body,
pleasure. I can love me all of me now. only love no punishment
no need to suffer.
self-love is good. feeling my past is good. feeling my now is
good. expressing myself is good.
I want to succeed. emotionally personally professionally. I want
success unencumbered by punishment free to love and yes

sep 02 / 91
I felt sad crying on my way home. still. crying for me for all
I do. for all I've done. for all I am. why cry? I should feel happy,
shouldn't I?
no. it's the loss I weep for. the fading away of the old me. the
familiar that's no longer.
inside I sense a drop of clear fresh pure magic water. it's me I
know. a bear always knows where the water is. now it's a matter
of letting the drop flow through me. feel me. I will do it. yes I

sep 06 / 91
I feel cocooned. warm and silky unique unusual. I want to cry
out cry in my difference. I want to celebrate my difference. polish
myself to life. I want to like me who I am writer. so many women
struggle. so many silent women. who writes meaning is shunned
and shunted.
trying to hold time in its place. time and space have broken apart,
have pushed against one another until I'm wandering back and
forth back and forth in and out in and out
I'll do it. I'll find my balance. time, my darling, time.

WAYNE: You haven't taken your anger out.
ME: Catharsis is not my style.

sep 17 / 91
my head is full. full full full. foil. slow down, beckylane.
relax.

The most unfortunate thing is that the victims are so often
accused of making all this up. The victims end up being suspects,
and the suspects end up being the victims. That's a real travesty.
People say children invent these stories after watching TV,
but before there was any media coverage of these cases, the
allegations these kids made were extremely consistent with the
allegations other kids were making in other parts of the country.
These kids weren't networking with each other. Nobody was
talking about it. Children don't make up stories like these.

— Sandi Gallant

Behind bad luck comes good luck.

long lines, clean and syllabic as knotted bamboo. Yes!

— Phyllis Webb

and me, I slowly gather together the strips of my past. a past
I don't want and in many ways I can't accept. where is the lie?
where is the truth? in the strips.

in the past, I prescribed my own drugs to heal me, not out of love but out of knowing wisdom incredible ability to perceive detail. I've been an object to myself. other. do this, it will be good for me. this is how I can take care of myself. it works. it almost always works.
but love? did I do it out of self-love? no. never. it never occurred to me to love myself. denied the self-hate the loathing, what else could I do?
now I've begun to love myself.

and my dad? he rocked me held me sang to me told me I was special

                    raped me

and my mother? she wouldn't touch me. stiffened if I got too close. moved away. pushed me away. ran away. I don't remember even holding my mother's hand much until she was dying her wanting me to hold her hand large clammy disease stench left on my hands for what seemed always because I saw her almost daily and the smell didn't really go away.
the absence of nurture is supposed to somehow right itself through the magic of touch. touch is such an important bonding. love touches feels through touch

                    mother's touch

four   flannel pajamas   barefoot
smells so good so clean from bathing
                              wood on my soles the floor
sometimes warm sometimes cool
no no mommy   just come and you'll see I'll hold your hand
I'll hold your hand gentle smooth my mommy loves me yes she
does my mommy loves me
                              down the hall my mommy's
bedroom my daddy's too dark and grey air smoky cigarettes
musty smells of drunk makes me feel sick then there he is my
dad his face so red and shaking all over
                              see honey it's just your daddy
having fun your daddy loves us special
                    I'll hold your hand   you'll see
numb
        feel only mommy's hand the floor the smell the
                                        numb
over and over and over not loud but scary me not me it's not
me it's him he's red and my little angel my little angel
you're my little angel aren't you yes you are my little
angel you're daddy's little angel
                    numb
just watch just watch just sit sitting at the head of the
bed daddy's face large red purple spitting look at me look
at daddy look at daddy yes yes daddy's little angel
                              mommy too look at mommy honey look
at mommy happy happy
                                        scared

sep 18 / 91

I would go to my bed afterwards. my parents quiet me knowing I can go now smell good. knowing it wasn't over. knowing I would get the douche. sometimes that night. sometimes the next day. or the next. over and over again.

no mommy no mommy mommy   how does it feel cunt
you like it this way   eh
daddy's little angel eh   you like it
little angels die young yes they do you like it
                                  bitch

sep 19 / 91

endless this money stress. everyone wants money — half my
funds have to go for fees and books and still the government
wants 25% for rent. that leaves me with about a thousand dollars
four months' food and car and kids. waiting in line for handouts.
why am I doing this? for some future security? paying back loans
until I die? I want an easier life. I'm sick of it. three jobs a bank
loan visa to its limit. and the stress of grad work on top of two
kids to feed what kind of a world is this? what? a working-classer
in grad school? try it, sucker. try it. they don't even know what
poverty is, the middle class. no concept. none. some intellectual
theory of

she was such a sad little girl. all that sadness.

sep 21 / 91

obstacles. I've had enough for a whole team of women. I've
proved myself, okay? I've suffered incest ritual abuse hate from
my mother rejection from my family baby in my youth a baby
who died abusive husband custody dispute abusive former
husband who just won't quit lost my house my car my job. I
won't forget, okay?
is it so much to ask? what? do I have a tattoo? pick me pick me

---

for misery. I've had it. I'm sick of it. there's nothing wrong with me. I don't deserve to go through life this way. I don't carry a dark cloud of doom.

sep 22 / 91

my mother believed it. she believed I'm innately evil and I deserve constant punishment I should constantly atone for this evil which I somehow carry with me like a spell. I've perfected calm in the face of fucking doom, okay? I know how to keep going keep working toward something better keep throwing back the obstacles. big muscles, no trouble. I've had to struggle so much I tell bits of my life and people turn tail. I want a better life for me and my kids. is it so much to ask?

                              and me? can I be
                         intimate outside abuse?
                         yes. my kids. my friends.

SAMANTHA: I wish every morning was like this, Mom. Crawling into your warm bed with you. You always smell so good. Then just hanging around with you like this. Feels great, Mom.

---

sep 23 / 91

opposites. inside, I believe my past. outside, I don't. outside,
I believe my present. I live it, after all. inside, though, I don't
believe it. does this make sense? I think so. my inside wants my
outside to believe. my outside wants my inside to believe. the
disbelief inside comes from the past. unable to believe without
present belief. without acceptance. how can my present
perceptions be okay without accepting the past? they can't.
I need to dance with myself my life with love and understanding.
let go of doubt self-doubt. I believe my past most of the time.
I believe my present most of the time. time, my love. time.

You see, my "inside me" could shut everything off but there was
still my body and it had its own life "outside" of "me inside." It
is my outside that really knows. It's my eyes that saw, my mouth
that felt, spoke, and took in; my arms, they have memories too.
Before I can let my inside "me" remember, my body's memories
have to come out.

— Michelle Smith (a pseudonym)

Where your treasure is, there will your heart be also.

sep 24 / 91

I want to cradle my past in my present. shame shadows me when the past seeps through. why must it seep? why not just be there bold? no shame. shame silences me. unconscious conviction that I'm worthless it'll show through it's showing through. silence. shame. I'm self-engulfed in shame. I don't have to be. I can get out, I know. I'm often out. no shame. no thought to it. power is internal. always internal.

sep 26 / 91

sometimes I wish I was one of my kids. I don't confuse with shame in their eyes. shame is a noun and a verb. a painful mental feeling aroused by wrongdoing. a wrongdoing intended to arouse shame. that's pretty much how my parents and partners operated. shame solicitation

sep 27 / 91

I was once a little girl. I was abused beyond

    I've come a long and long way. I want to open my book without fear and shame. I know I'll do it. my in and my out. my past and my present. I know I'll do it.

sep 29 / 91

feel good right just right about grad school. the learning works its way. it's all in there, says stephanie, points to her temple with her index finger. even if you think you've forgotten.

A DREAM: two days running. eyes closed but able to see to drive even. trying to open my eyes. I can't see my eyes won't open. I can't open them. yet I can and indeed am seeing. when I'm finally able to open my eyes in the dream, I have glasses to wear during sleep. to see my inside out

sep 30 / 91

still not ready to believe my past. still I resist.

there's something I haven't remembered. something looming.
something to do with my dad and shoe polish silver polish
the basement of the house where I grew up my father's role
as teacher. expecting him to teach to help me to see. not there.
my daddy's not there. I'm lost and I can't see. help me daddy
help me.

the fear that I may be wrong. I know I'm not. I know. how
could he be so nice so horrible?

to look back and in. it's all in there.

learning to love me all of me the me I cannot see. I have my
glasses. I want to see. I will. me.

I'm so scared. so scared and so happy at the same time. this
last memory   it's so hard being me

Hope for the best, but prepare for the worst.

oct 02 / 91
I have glasses to wear in my sleep. I saw them.
my dad was disguised in my dreams in the past. still. that
brutal man was and is my dad. in the past, I felt no anger
no fear nothing when I encountered the stranger my dad in my
dreams. I was often surprised, disturbed that I had dreams
where the content was alarmingly grotesque and frightening,
they should have been nightmares I should have woken up
filled with fear but I wasn't. didn't.

oct 04 / 91
I won't find my dad. I have no dad. he's a monster. he beguiles.
covers up. sweeps the path clean behind him. no evidence. that's
why he's so hard for me to find. I keep looking for the obvious.
but he's the opposite. he's not obvious. nothing about him is
obvious. what shows is not the full picture. it's confusing and
outside reason. within reason, he could trick. become someone
else, whatever he wanted. able to reshape reality for real. so
much so that I had to choose. the monster or the sensitive man.

oct 05 / 91

actions. actions/words and not words alone define reality.
my dad was astoundingly abusive in our love relationship.
his way is silence. if there are no words the behaviour
doesn't exist. and to ensure safety, bury it inside the vastness of
the psyche. lots of room there.

oct 06 / 91

why am I telling all of this to her? to my counsellor? what does it
mean? where will it go?
out the window and lost in the view. in the trees in the museum
now downtown in the wind among the high-rises some falling
into the river travels east to who knows where. I've never before
been heard or listened to most of the time loved too from some
perch me a precious flower my scent margaret's to

I was afraid that I would learn to love myself mechanically
in therapy. still am. machine-love at me-machine. that if my
counsellor didn't soften like her eyes her hands her hold, I
would succeed in therapy I would learn how to take care of
myself in power but it would be like before. cold wisdom.
structured love. constructed and all the foundations showing
bold. aesthetically crafted. intellectual concept of self-love no
emotional bond.
that's my longing: my love for me.

oct 15 / 91

I came across a photograph while researching. a child sitting
behind a barbed wire fence. the child sits like I did, knees v'd
behind. barbed wire. I survived it.

oct 16 / 91

when I saw the picture I had a gut sick sinking feeling had to sit
down. experienced myself sitting there again and again. scared.
waiting. I wish I could remember more about what I was thinking. I read about women who remember what they were thinking
saying to themselves. I just seem to remember how I felt and
from a distance. my first reaction is a kind of disbelief the
feelings there the picture there me there, but how could it be?
how could I have completely forgotten?
knowing many women do and even understanding why but still
for me I keep wanting more. other women have memories of how
they felt about the future when they were small. I have no past is
still how I feel. nothing to draw on except these visual-feeling
memories one after the other so

I think

if I could remember some thoughts I could avoid feeling
devastated about so much now. maybe more time. maybe making
it through the memories will open up more space.
right now I feel maternal toward my self my past. connected
because it seems to fit. otherwise I would have to label
myself in some way pathological. my steps seem so small
sometimes. mystery of myself. myself. me.

It would seem to me that since children quite literally all over the world are independently disclosing very specific details of quite bizarre abuse — details they could not possibly have fantasised — either we have a massive international conspiracy of toddlers or else there's some form of intelligent adult organisation involved.

— Pamela S. Hudson [b]

he takes me downstairs like always but this time he lets my
dog come   she sometimes tries to but he won't let her
              she understands me
              she knows I'm sad after even though he tells me
  I'm lucky
                    I'm special
this time he calls her   she's scared   I'm scared too
my dad is mean to her   he laughs and plays sometimes but
sometimes he beats her too   she doesn't trust him
when he's kind
                  he takes us both downstairs
         I'm supposed to clean and polish all the shoes
I like the way they look when they're all shined and lined
up in a row on the newspaper
                  I put them in order of size
                  sometimes colour
                  sometimes girls and boys

oct 20 / 91
four days since writing about my dog. had a dream this morning.

A DREAM: in this dream I'm a man. I work for the government. mr. stern is my name. no first name. no other life. I even think somewhere, laughing (not me mr. stern, but me dream critic aware it's a dream, symbolic), that the name's like the hero of some russian realist novel. probably significant if I think about the meaning symbolic in the russian novel. mr. stern never goes anywhere. he lives and works in the dark. never goes out where it's light.

oct 20 / 91

I threw out the last vestige of memory material. the bag full of
shoe polish and such that's been in the cupboard since I moved in
over a year ago. never unpacked. the rest of the memory is here.
waiting to surface. I know I was eleven. I know it's when he
stopped fucking me. just like that. I know he killed my dog to
"teach" me not to tell.

oct 21 / 91

this is around the time I started to go to the river more. peace.
the loss was almost too much. the noise of the water allowed me
to remember something. loud loud. I didn't know what the
"something" was but I was drawn to water for years. still.
the something was hope. I believed in good when I was at the
river. the smell the warm the wet. I cried a lot. for me. for my
dog. I hated my dad. I wished he was dead. my body shut down
and I forgot I'd had sex with my dad. I forgot about my dog. that
I'd had a dog. that I'd had a past.

oct 24 / 91

I've been reading about shame. margaret asked was it shame
I felt when I couldn't speak. I said, no. what then? pain, for sure.
but when I read about the physiological indicators of shame,
I exhibit many. most. the defense mechanisms that fit: denial. with
margaret, I don't feel the shame. I believe I'm experiencing

oct 25 / 91

my conclusion: yes, I'm experiencing profound shame when I attempt, and indeed do, talk to margaret about my past. but I don't feel it. I know what shame feels like. I feel shame, the feeling of shame, I spiral into shame frequently. it. shame.
I identify so profoundly with my past and with my father that I feel responsible for my own abuse. that somehow I caused it deserved it inflicted it even. my shame is all but all-encompassing. in fact, in order not to feel that shame I had to resee the world around me. the past I now remember doesn't fit with the past I didn't remember. in fact, it's so different so as to be, at first, not believable. now, though I believe it some of the time and though these new memories are certainly more congruous with my family's present reality, with it comes both the realization of the enormousness of my personal shame and, incredibly, a shame for that shame.
shit. one step at a time.

Remember, there are big changes for you,
but you will be happy.

oct 26 / 91

shit. no interest in food. having to make myself eat.
I'm so rigid stiff closed inward self-protective. I don't know
what it's like to be nurtured. I know how to nurture. even
myself I'm getting really good at it. but there's a huge gap.
I keep so much of myself to myself. I take care of myself, but not
out of love unconditional because my self-love is actually very
conditional. it's based on shame and some intellectual idea of
what's good for me. no value, really, just some sense of positivity.
I'm ashamed of my own wisdom. I'm ashamed of my methods of
self-help. I'm ashamed to share them because they seem so
goody-two shoes. and idealistic. utopian even. but they work. I
want to value myself.

oct 27 / 91

my dog must have died some other way. she must have been run
over or something.

my dad had a knife had that look on his
face like at that place when he watched them hurt me at that
place
scary look   happy and mean and red face and
slash slash blood my sandie's dead she's dead her mouth
open her eyes gone rolled away into her head she squeaks
my dad says if you tell anyone and I mean anyone cunt
you're dead
you cunts are all the same
fucking cunt   no more tail for you
you're a cunt now   no one   you hear cunt   no one

oct 28 / 91
I want to feel loved when I hurt.

oct 29 / 91
I want to feel loved by someone when I'm hurting. to let out
some of the pain and get it back but changed. changed
colour. changed colour so I feel worthy.

> *I want to hold my dog*
scared
> *shaking shaking cold*
>> *I want my sandie*
shaking   rocking   crying

oct 30 / 91

margaret tells me how important it is for me to hear myself talk.
to speak out my diary, not to myself, but to others and to her.
to hear my memories out of my mouth with my ears.

oct 31 / 91

people say, you're doing so well. wow!
what's the rush? why do you push yourself so hard?
because I was pushed so hard, damn it. because I was beaten and
raped and fucked and humiliated and my memory of it all is like a
fucking video. it's here for my viewing but not for my showing. I
want to show it, damn it. I want to show it.
what? I don't know. write on and on and on. spend inordinate
amounts of time alone. a loner. what? don't know. why is it too
hard to tell anyone? haven't told anyone about my dog.

haen't tld anyne aout m
n't old one out
ave d oe
hold
have

don't tell don't tell don't tell cunt cunt you're just a
cunt now then later after at supper what's happened nothing
everything's normal can't eat no appetite no thank you I'm
not hungry dad's here normal dad sitting in his chair
watching the news picking his nose big nostrils big fingers
rolling his nose bits between his thumb and forefinger
falling asleep he's tired he works hard he's my dad I love
him he loves me

                        he'd never hurt me that's for sure
he's nice   he drives me places   he laughs and he's funny
with my friends   sings when he's drunk

                                                dances fun

god ym tuoba enoyna dlot t'nevah

the child is the mirror for the adult.
had you seen me as a child, you would have seen an incredibly
sad and withdrawn child. a child who learned to live alone among
many people. alone.

nov 13 / 91
I've made it all up. he didn't take me to a farm. he didn't
make me do those things. he didn't fuck me at home. he
didn't teach me how to have sex. he didn't kill my dog. he
didn't rape kids and animals. I've made the whole thing up.
that's why I can't connect with it, truly engage with it.
because none of it happened. I'm just some deluded doodoo.
doudou. doowa doowa.
move in and out and through. write myself from one feeling
to another so pliable so malleable. what?

STEPHANIE: This is a big one: the scenario for most women who are raised in abusive homes is, they grow up, get married, have children, abuse them, and then come to realize it's wrong. Why are you different? What possessed that little girl to behave another way? What kept her going? What?

ME: That little girl was me. I am she. And I'm not so sure I can answer that question. What allows anyone to perceive something different? Something better? Creativity? Chance? Psychoanalysts are just as baffled as any of the rest of us. My parents were very religious. Hard to believe, I know. But I remember hearing bits read out in church. I believed it, took it with me, do unto others as you would have them do unto you, jesus loves me yes I know. It made more sense than

this frightened little girl is afraid of all adults except aunty sahara. she's safe. she's okay. I can see it in her eyes in the way she looks at me the way she talks to me the way she silently opens up a space for me. here, honey, here's your safe space. you can come into it whenever you want. if you want. not words just a gesture of body of place in the air.

all these layers of protection I've built up around myself.
layer after layer after layer. almost forty years of layers.

You have an ability to sense and know higher truth.

nov 13 / 91
I worked hard all week all today I wept for me. alone but okay.
I'll be okay. it'll take a while but I'll do it. so alone. still haven't
been able to tell anyone about my dog

nov 13 / 91
alone

My mother's otherwise ordinary middle-class family participated in one of these secret satanic cults. We lived in a small city, but our Saturday nights were regularly spent at explicitly satanic cult meetings held in a cabin in the country, a site the cult owned specifically for ritual purposes. I can trace the family's involvement back to my grandmother's generation at the very least, although it probably goes back further.

— Elizabeth S. Rose

women still needed to be discreetly free of
unwanted babies
lower-class
people and those guilty
of sexual indiscretions
were delegated to the
ranks of the damned

— Martin H. Katchen

hence, satanic
practices continue to exist in the late
twentieth century

nov 18 / 91
shame. shame for what? accepting a definition of myself
as worthless and deserving of being treated with hatred and
disdain.

If you can't win, shoot for a tie.

as the writer just keeps on writing. all this writing all intended
to help me get past a powerful resistance a silence I still haven't
gotten past. I think I know some of the reasons why now. it's
simple, actually, and I haven't been able to get beyond it, into it:
I deserve to be loved.

ANNETTE (grew up in an upper-middle-class town in the Midwest): I was what they called a "breeder." I was less than twelve years old. They overpowered me and got me pregnant and then they took my babies. They killed them right in front of me.

nov 23 / 91
the unconscious is a reader. she reads in her own way in her own language.
wanting wishing to feeling better. how to? what to? I'm so tired of feeling shitty. of feeling inward. fuck. what? don't know.
thought on my way home, now too, it'd be so much easier just to be dead.

Usually, when one writes of oneself it is called non-fiction — I disbelieve that. Hindsight is always slightly ficticious.
— Lee Maracle

A SCHOLAR: I don't know. Do you really think it's wise to use your name and your father's name in here? Wouldn't it be better to call it autofiction or something like that? At least to change the names. Then you wouldn't have to worry about lawsuits, you know? The law is very frightening and very powerful. Aren't you afraid of the possibility of that process?

ME: The decision has been made for me. I can't publish unless I use a pseudonym. My father and men like him are the ones who're very frightening and very powerful. They're more powerful than the law because the law protects people like them before it protects people like me. Torture defies language, destroys memory. What I'm proposing here when I put words to my torture is termed allegation by law. Implicit in allegation is "unproven." The "proving" is the responsibility of a third party who's equipped with the language of law, which maintains a certain reassuring distance from reality, a critical correctness of the rational and the analytical. How can this be "proven" almost forty years after the fact? I was too young to even know where I was and I was forced to stay under a blanket in the back of the car during the long ride there. The people there were strangers to me. Babies' and children's bodies were sometimes burned sometimes not, then buried with rotting potatoes in remote farm fields. Are we going to wait for the unearthing of the "proof"? Who'll be delegated to do the digging and where?

nov 25 / 91
told margaret, finally, about my dog.
it was too much to process, she says.
what happened to you when you were young, that was
dangerous, she says.
she asks, what do you feel when you can't talk?
fear, I say.
and is it because you can't tell the secret?
it doesn't get that far. it's just fear.

Libel.   A method of defamation expressed by print, writing,
pictures, or signs. In its most general sense, any publication that
is injurious to the reputation of another. A false and unprivileged
publication in writing of defamatory material. Bright v. Los
Angeles Unified School Dist., 51 Cal.App.3d 852, 124 Cal.Rptr.
598, 604
    . . . Malice must be proved on a showing that defendant
published material either knowing it to be false or recklessly
without regard as to whether it is true or false. N. Y. Times v.
Sullivan, 376 U.S. 254, 84 S.Ct. 710, 11 L.Ed.2d 686.
                              — *Black's Law Dictionary*, 5th Edition

I want to feel smooth like music in water
a good poem

BECKYLANE'S BROTHER: Here you are just trying to blame all your troubles on our father. Sure I got hit a little too hard for what I did sometimes, but it seems to me I remember sitting down to three square meals a day. You must really think you're something special, eh? As far as I'm concerned, I no longer have a sister named Beckylane.

nov 26 / 91
open like a flower. listen to my soft. I can accept nurture. I can ask for nurture. such a long way I've come.

dec 05 / 91
so. one day on oneanother. last night I imagined me the little girl who was abused. so hard. so much. but I did it.
this morning driving in my car my left hand small my child hand dried orange blood sticky then just my hand my adult hand on the steering wheel.
maybe if I could talk to other women who've been through simi-lar experiences, maybe it would help — so all alone not lonely but isolated so hard.
I've read about other women but my life is another kind of reading.
listen to your body, beckylane. your body my
body

My body is my only clue. It's the only thing I couldn't compro-
mise or rationalize. It was there. My mind and feelings could go
away but my body was there and had to be there the whole time.
— Michelle Smith

a silence inside
smooth like morning water trees sky
can't tell where the shore is
in a canoe
still water still air still me

dec 10 / 91

when I went upstairs after my dad killed my dog, I watched him
in his chair. he looked so normal, as if nothing had happened. I
was stunned, horrified that he could do that. act as though nothing had happened. I started to think about all the nice things he'd
done recently. in the past when my mother abused me I did the
same thing. I remembered all the nice things she'd done.

dec 11 / 91

sometimes I thought about the nice things about my mother when
I was being beaten or raped at that farm. I would feel better.
sometimes I went far away.
time seems so slow. such an emotional struggle. I'm okay. I
haven't dropped out of anything but it takes so much energy
to stay on the positive side and consequently other things
have to give. my appetite. exercise.
margaret asks me if I censor what I tell her there. no, I say.
my past isn't censorship. it's a muteness.
oh, how I want success. let it out, honey me. let it come out.
no one can hurt me now. I really am a big girl now.
now, when I'm in an intense emotional situation, I don't react
until later when I'm alone. I feel the feelings but only by myself.
then there's no interaction. it's all one way. I don't choose, I just
do. I want to be able to choose whether or not to interact. I want
to choose what I want. conscious choice. not unconscious
reaction. I can choose whether or not I want to read a book.
take a bath. get my hair cut.

dec 12 / 91
words caught in my throat. respect myself hate myself think
I'm a liar wish I felt better when will song be in me
laughter joy contentment acceptance pain sorrow. doing it
alone no family no one to cry
cocooned and not. hugging myself.
somehow I have to break out. sticky and safe and warm and
light/bright in here but I'm too inward. I want to share.
beckylane.
pain. such pain where to let it go? how?

Words cannot describe this process. It is felt knowledge, a
private universe of sentient being and it separates us from the
external world and draws spider webs of silk between our
personal universe and the people who nurture us.

— Lee Maracle

READERS: We discussed trying to work more of a feminist perspective into the narration, one example being more mention of women friends who were supportive, less emphasis on one person (your counsellor) being the only important person in your healing.

SALLY: I had no idea you were going through so much. I mean, you talked about it, but still, I had no idea. You're so strong so   silent
ME: I don't know what to say. I tried to tell you more try to tell you more about how I feel how I felt. I feel like I need to be held. But I can't ask. Does the child ask to be held? The child in me won't share her feelings no she won't, without body/words both. My parents said they loved me. But their bodies

dec 15 / 91
reading a book on incest realize I've read most of it before. there's a small section, only a couple of paragraphs, on ritual abuse. those words. ritual abuse. so hard to see those words. I'd go inside into another reality. my reality where I was me another me, lane. she was always kind always nice. we played. we talked. she talked mostly and I mostly listened. she was very wise calm clean. she answered really hard questions even when I was a lot older than her/me. I knew she was me too. after

my dad killed my dog when I was eleven she went away. she was too sad to come home. I was really alone then.

BECKYLANE'S REPORT CARD, AGE 11: Beckylane is an industrious and conscientious student. She never leaves work incomplete. She is pleasant and co-operative — a fine all-round student. Good creative and artistic ability. I should like to see her considering something in this field as her future career.

Answer just what your
heart prompts you.

dec 15 / 91
afraid I'm like my dad. a fucking fake.
I know how to love. how to feel. him too. but he is poison.
maybe I'm poison too. maybe I'm poison too and I just don't
know it I'm blind to it like he is. he thinks he's nice. so
do his friends. his neighbours. his family.
no. that's not it. I'm okay. nice and not. not and nice.
depends. I do love without abuse. I know I do. my kids. my
friends. but my lovers

dec 17 / 91
another day another
read the rest of the book. bleak. talks about the positive strengths
of children becoming the negative disorders of adults. why not
use the creative strengths as ways to conduct adult therapy?
the little girl in me wants to feel safe. she needs me with her in
order to do this. all of me. she needs me to hold her out bold.
out. how to hold and love "disorder"?
on the outside.
nothing to say
my childhood was dictated to me. no choice. violence. hate. rape.
no childhood. adult skills. control. survival. how to survive.

my instinct is to nurture. nurture is nine-tenths instinct. it is a
giving. a giving without return.
I have an inner wisdom. I've often listened to it but the picture I
have had of myself has been distorted. my picture is coming
clearer and clearer and into focus

mauve green blue

Having been born into an intergenerational familial satanic
cult, my abuse began at less than one month of age and
continued until my early twenties when I left the home of my
parents. I was also abused in a much larger cult group, which
had at times approximately 100 people present for major
ceremonies. My abuse occurred in Manitoba, Ontario, and the
United States, in various locations, including homes, churches,
beaches, campgrounds, warehouses, and graveyards.

— Amethya

dec 18 / 91
I feel suicidal. I have to keep reminding myself that
I haven't worked this hard to give up but
living two different lives like when I was young. in one
life I'm capable, competent, marking, writing, teaching,
learning, working, mothering.
in the other, I'm terrified.
I'm trying to make my past mine in the real world to make my
past my present too. I'm so terrified.
the more I remember, the more I remember. chanting chanting
fiddles happy music so much terror. I feel panicked and anxious
what if someone finds out they'll stick sticks into me all over
they'll kill me no I want to die.
I want to live, damn it
I look at myself and I'm amazed at my stamina at my success
as a woman from poverty pain powerlessness. at my success as
a mother in spite of my own mother. this kid inside has
taught me well. and I've listened and believed. she was my
mother my role model. I was my mother.
come on out, kid. come on out. it's okay it's safe I know it's safe
intellectually. but emotionally, I don't feel safe. no I don't.

dec 19 / 91
so what am I going to do? hope I can last four days before I
see margaret? read several articles on ritual abuse yesterday
something I probably couldn't have done before yesterday. and
what a stupid thing to do memories flooding back yes they did

this no they didn't do that I'm lucky they didn't do that.
I have a strong urge, a command, to kill myself. I want to think I
should almost couldn't make myself get into my car to drive
home. trying to use the skills I used when I was a kid, want to
deny suppress it's not that bad it's not that bad I'm here now no
one can hurt me. over and over.
beckylane. phone margaret. tell her what's happening maybe she
can help. let her try.
no. I can do this by myself.
why?
shame. she'll think I'm weak. she'll think I'm lying.
let her decide. she can only help, beckylane. do it. phone
margaret. tell her what's happening. the terror. the flashes.
the knowing.
knowing what? that it happened, damn it. that yes my dad abused
me raped me beat me. dressed in a dress like the priest wore.
something covering his head his face a hood and something
covering his face. I knew it was him his smell the music in his
voice. no. this is not my daddy my daddy loves me.
they told me I was evil. marked. a third eye they could see it
everyone who knows can see it.
so I looked down. always look down so no one will see you. no.
I'm not bad. I can look up. god loves me loves children best.

you're the devil's child   see this   see
                                    I can't write it
                                                            six
          six
                    six
                                        you're the devil's cunt

In each of the five cases, ritual abuse was indeed occurring. It is very sad to report that to date the children in four of the five cases have not been protected from the alleged perpetrators. These alleged perpetrators retain unsupervised visitation rights. Unbelievably, in one case involving two children, the *non*perpetrator parent is restricted to supervised visits and monitored phone calls, while the perpetrator parent has full custody. All efforts by the nonperpetrator parents to protect their children have been met by resistance from the child protection agencies and the judicial system.

— Linda Stone and David Stone

that baby's going to die
she's too big swollen purple shiny
blood
there's rope on my wrists
hanging shoulders arms hurting
hurting

Does the child report being tied by ropes, wires or cables, hung from hooks, placed in closets, spread over an inverted pentagram or an inverted cross?

Why is the major ritual in one of the predominant religions in our culture a symbolic act of cannibalism [where] millions of Christians symbolically ingest the blood and body of Jesus Christ every Sunday?

— Gail Fisher-Taylor

dec 21 / 91

almost three hours with margaret. I can do this. I'm going to live. I was completely beside myself when I first met with her. suicidal beyond reason. I would have had to take serious measures had we failed to communicate. I was prepared even to admit myself to hospital on condition of no drugs. no choice. I was ordered to die. brainwashed. die. die. had to use everything I had to stay here no don't it's over go talk to margaret.

reading the material gave me an understanding of my lack of trust. of my feelings for margaret. don't tell. tell and die. I had the picture in my head. violent death. die. highway embankment. works. warm. dead.

I was out of it. I have to talk to you, I said. you asked me if I censor what I tell you and I said I don't. I don't. but there's so much I don't tell you. it's not censorship censor implies choice.

I'm not choosing. intellectually, I know I should be able to trust you but emotionally, who am I trusting? I don't know anything about you. on and on back and forth. she said, what would make you feel safe?
I said, that you believe me. she said, I believe that everything you've told me about what happened to you when you were young, happened to you.

I'm ready to trust. I'm ready to risk whatever might happen. I don't think I'll be disappointed but I don't know. I want to risk it.

10 Reasons Why I Would Falsely Accuse My Parents of Incest or Ritual Abuse

> 7. I felt left out and wanted desperately to belong somewhere.
>
> 6. I wanted to be disbelieved and called a "liar" by every "respected" newspaper, talk show and radio interviewer, "expert," "scholar," "lawyer," "friend," and family member.
>
> — Jezanna Rainforest

dec 22 / 91
keep on writing, beckylane. so fucking hard. the pull to death is
almost too much. your life will fall apart. you'll see. kill yourself
first you'll see. misery will be yours. you are cursed. born cursed.
die.
die while you can. you'll regret life.

If at first you don't succeed, borrow some
money and try again.

dec 22 / 91
no. I'm going to talk. talk and remember talk and re member. until I see myself whole again. if I have to sleep, I'll sleep. if I have
to not eat, I'll make sure I eat at least once a day. good food. it
helps to eat with someone else so I'll do that as often as I can. if I
have to not exercise, I won't. it's not good for an abused body
anyway. I'd probably get sick or hurt.
tell margaret everything you can, beckylane. she can only help.
tell your close friends. they can only help.
I wish this was all over. that I could just live my life.

You should not return to the past to revive an
old relationship.

Ritually victimized children's problems with death follow logically from
        Ritually victimized children may experience problems with certain colors
           Ritually abused children often develop one or more problems with eating
           Ritually abused children may display marked anxiety in the form of
          Ritually abused children may develop a variety of speech disorders in
           The ritually abused child may exhibit "flat" affect and fail to respond to
        Ritually abused children often exhibit attentional

                — Catherine Gould

dec 23 / 91

beckylane. margaret's the first person you've dared to try to trust on a level which is real. you take yourself seriously as a mother but you don't take the trust of your children seriously because you give it little value. margaret asked, were your children a reason for life, a consideration, and you said, no. why is that? because you don't understand your importance to your children's beings. you don't value yourself.

          I want to but it seems skewed. it seems like every time I dare to value myself things blow up in

my face. like the essay. like with margaret too. so much depends upon this woman.
that's okay. that's realistic you know that from your reading. the essay? you made a mistake. womanwriting in that manworld. there'll be reasonable options. you'll see.

help wipe the blood off my hands instead of running from it, or standing there in awe and shock

— Shirley Turcotte [a]

WILHELMINA: I remember going to a party with you sometime around the time when you were struggling to stay alive. I had no idea how bad it was. I would have liked to have heard more from you. Still would. Do you really think it's fair for your friends that you keep so much to yourself?
ME: Right now I feel like everyone I'm close to wants me to be everything. Always a piece missing

Your road will be made smooth for you by good friends.

———

dec 23 / 91
my dad was disguised in my dreams. likewise, he was
disguised at that farm. by subsequently "loving" me oh so
tenderly, he "proved" to me that he would never hurt me he
never hurt me on that farm he'd stopped going. I believed
him, of course. he would take care of me all my life. his
angel. a child of the devil. cursed. my mother afraid of me.
fear and respect and love and hate.

dec 23 / 91
feeling so stressed alone resisting. think, okay, are you
going to say goodbye to the kids? it's inevitable you know.
you are well programmed.

the more you remember the more you
tell the closer you'll be to death ha
ha ha you think you're stronger than
evil you idiot save yourself the
trouble they won't believe you they
may say they do but they don't

dec 23 / 91

bullshit. I want life. I want happiness. I deserve it. fuck off you assholes from my past. you are evil. I'm not. period.

dec 23 / 91

you can do it, beckylane, you can do it. you can do it. think of the woman from _____ , she did it you can do it. wrap christmas presents. in the present. you can do it. smell something familiar and safe. stay here, honey. stay here. cry. stay here. for gregory and samantha. stay.

dec 24 / 91

margaret thinks I want her to rescue me. I don't. oh, I'm in such a mess. I don't want to be rescued. I want to be heard. to hear. to trust. to stop being so afraid. I'm so strong. I know I am and the irony is, my own strength makes it that much harder for me to believe my own past. believe it, beckylane. belief will bring more strength. more courage. I want to, I'm close.
liar. liar liar liar. what are you trying to prove?
trust. I *have* to trust myself. to believe what I don't understand. the whole. the whole says, yes.

listen to the rhythm of your own music, beckylane. sing yourself
whole. if we weren't strong enough we wouldn't have come this
far. you know that. fly, my love. fly.
the abuse of a thousand summers. what is that repulsive voice?
where does it come from?
programmed, my love. we were programmed. forced to stay.
hung by the wrists.

                                                          stay   cunt
          fucking listen you little fuck
          think ya can get away with something do ya
          you're nothin but a piece of shit   make no mistake
you die if you tell   hear
                                                          fucking dead

               repeat it again   cunt
                                I promise
          I will love my god

                              I will not defile the earth
                                        with my filth
                              I am of the devil
                              I am evil

          fuckin say it   cunt
            ain't nobody gonna save ya
               think daddy's gonna save ya   do ya
               fuckin stupid kid
                    I'm fuckin runnin this show and you fuckin
                                             die kid

          we're tryna save ya   cunt
          say it   see this
          this is what's fuckin written all over you ya filth
          the devil
          I see it every time I look at your fuckin face

six

    spits in my face   *six*
    pees on me
    rubs it in my face my eyes my nose my mouth

                         six

dec 24 / 91
I'm making it up.

no   I can see his face   oh

dec 24 / 91
I'm making it up.
why?
I'm crazy. whatever. I'm crazy. totally bonkers looloo.
no. I'm opening myself up to my past. stop now, beckylane.
slow down. it'll all come let it come more slowly. don't push.
it's too much too fast. you'll never make any sense out of
any of it. it's not sense.

what do I see? me. flying still no body. I'm so tired. this is so
hard. I'm so poor. no money. I'm so tired. I want to
I want to laugh. to sing. to play I want to

You will gain money by a
speculation or lottery.

I want to cry out my agony to

dec 24 / 91
still here. can write another essay.
still here. told stephanie what I'm going through.
still here. saw margaret. felt completely different. not
scared. first time. after all this time.
I need to believe my past.
learning trust. a new beginning.

dec 24 / 91
still here. stay grounded, beckylane. you're taking control
of your life, says margaret. quite the life. time. I need
time, and right now time is so slow. such a burden.
felt better after seeing margaret, though. safer somehow.
driving around looking for the place on the highway. looking
for the place. *no*

do it
rid the earth of your filth
do it
bless this earth
you will never go to heaven
you are filth
we are here to find you and rid the earth of the likes of
you
bless this earth

dec 24 / 91

I *have* to believe my past.

tired of feeling shitty. insidious long long dreams can't
remember any of it wake up feeling shitty I'm a fuck filth
why bother working so hard I'm only going to realize I'm shit.
trying to keep a picture of samantha so young so fresh so
vivacious so dependent. of gregory. knowing I've mothered
well, think big deal.

read through your diaries, says margaret. see how far you've
come. me so dependent on a woman I don't even know.
children don't fantasize themselves into victims, I've read.
but I am not a child. beckylane. it is our past. why do I resist
so strongly? what if my dad didn't do any of those things?
I mean, really didn't. what if I'm making it all up I really am
somehow evil. why do I resist?

it's not something you can talk about, says margaret. and
there is tremendous social pressure for disbelief.

I am so alone. taking my past with me and so alone. people
believe me but I don't believe myself. I want to feel good
about myself.

if I wasn't ready or if I couldn't do this, I wouldn't be doing it.
it's that simple. I am a strong woman. I have tremendous
strength. sally says, people force children to do such horrible
things and then make them think they're choosing. that they have
choice.

somehow I was made responsible or made to think I was
responsible for that baby's death.

I live my life being intellectually kind. no value on my own
behaviour no value on me. I need to value myself for real.

confused. why is it so easy so familiar just to hate myself? to behave well but take no credit? how else would one behave? so I'm smart. big deal.

dec 25 / 91
another memory looming. this memory needs trust. they convinced me I am evil I fought it all my life being kind and nurturing. I am ready for this. I am.

When you can't hear the unbearable or the unspeakable, when you can't believe what seems unbelievable, I'm once again alone. When I speak what seems unspeakable and you fall in the pain of it, I'm again silenced, because I don't want to hurt you — I only want to heal. When you can't hear without trying to fix or suggest or change my way of being with my memories, I'm again
— Shirley Turcotte [a]

Never give advice in a crowd.

BECKYLANE'S SISTER: Well, I don't really remember much of my childhood. The odd thing. I don't think it was that great, but I don't really want to remember. I remember when I was a teenager Mom told me to stay clear of you and I always stuck up for you. Mom and Dad just did the best they could, don't you think? It wasn't really that bad. Why do you want to drag up all that old stuff anyway? What's the point? Do you even have a reason? Mom's dead. Let the poor woman rest in peace. Dad's getting old. Just let him die in peace.

One possible explanation is that there are clever, ingenious perpetrators and that the police and social workers are not smart enough to penetrate their criminal conspiracy. We hear and read about allegations of double-decker graves and mobile crematoriums and trucks with cherry-pickers on them that will reach out over fences and pick up cattle that have been killed in ritual sacrifice. These are the clever, ingenious perpetrators that we're not smart enough to catch.

— FBI Special Agent Ken Lanning

But I say the following to those who say that [what Ken Lanning says] is true: That if it is true, this is the greatest criminal conspiracy ever to hit mankind. It makes the Mafia look like a bunch of pansies. Police have infiltrated every major crime conspiracy that has existed. They infiltrated Nazi Germany. British agents broke their codes in World War II. The Mediallin cartel in Colombia has been infiltrated. The FBI has been infiltrated. The KGB has been infiltrated. British Secret Service has been infiltrated.

— James Peters, National Center for the
Prosecution of Child Abuse

When a violent, gruesome movie or TV show attracts millions of viewers, this is considered normal behaviour, yet when survivors of ritual abuse speak out about having survived torture, ritual murder and repeated rapes, we are told it's not possible, that we must be either lying or crazy. This is what we are up against as ritual abuse survivors: a culture which disconnects us from feelings, from real, personal violence and its effects. From reality. And that disconnection, that disbelief, enables ritual abuse to continue without interference.

— Gail Fisher-Taylor

Avert misunderstanding by calm,
poise and balance.

If any man have an ear, let him hear. When the dragon saw that he was cast unto the earth, he persecuted the woman which brought forth the man child.

— Chant of High Satanic Priest
and/or
Holy Bible, Rev. 12.13, 13.9

it's all in the words

          well   *I might be uncomfortable*   *I say*
                                gets translated
           she says she'd feel hostile
I have a hard time with positive criticism   *I say*
                                gets translated
              she can't take negative criticism

in a day I can go through so much. I want to say, give it a rest. but it's been resting for nearly forty years and it wants to wake up. to wake up get up and move. I go back into self-hate and that's not where I want to be.

there are no easy answers no magic solution. sometimes I've pushed too hard. I want to push myself further and into that space where I believe I deserve to receive nurture. from me from others.

If we want to stop ritual abuse, the first step must be to believe that these brutal crimes occur. Society's denial makes recovery much more difficult for survivors. Those who have suffered from ritual abuse need the same respect and support that would be given to survivors of any tragedy.

— Elizabeth S. Rose

how to unengrain? how to do something there are no words for? me with my monologues with my words everywhere words that can't be seen or heard or felt. silence.

there's a huge wave of emotion inside me that wants to heal me. I can feel it caught here in my throat. but it doesn't surface. it's way way down underneath the surface how to get it here in the foam?

trying to push one silence through with another.

the water's warm today. smells good. wading. waiting.

the sand is warm
white with specks of black
if you use a magnet it makes long black fuzzy hairs
you can collect them in a jar   the sand at the river is best
see here from the long buggy grass
it's stiff and uncomfortable
here's where the rivers join
one skinny and fast   the other taking a break
here   put your feet in
it isn't warm it's cold but you get used to it
fuzzy foam   beige   loud

We're really on our own in this. People just don't want to know about it. When you tell them, and when they see you believe in the existence of satanic ritual abuse, you are attacked and attempts are made to discredit you. There are three major charges levelled. The first is that we just want fame and fortune. Alternatively we are accused of having a pathological preoccupation with the idea of ritual abuse. The third accusation is that we are all fundamentalist Christians, and therefore we're seeing the Devil everywhere.

— Pamela S. Hudson [b]

I'm trying to revalue my childhood. I'm trying to claim back my body from my past. in order to do that, I have to reperceive my childhood experiences and to relearn. unlearn and relearn. I placed all my love with my dad because as monstrous as he was, he showed love for me. understanding even. and I can't get past that and to what he really did to me. what my mother really did to me.
shit. this is so confusing.

why do you wear your socks in the water

what

I can't hear you

I've got a banana in my ear

dec 27 / 91
lost

I want to hold the bald fledgling. both hands cupped loving
warm gentle place inside the nest for mother's warm; for life.
my anxious hope for vision for me to see to be my power.

SAMANTHA: I love playing with you, Mom. You really know
how to play, did you know that?

A DREAM: many people around. some start to push through
a small door. a woman admitting people says to me, are you sure
you want to come in here? yes, I say. you're going to be involved
in the brutality in the violence? she asks. me: no. I just want to
watch.
in. hyper-bright colours all around. I know once I'm in there's
no way out. I'll stand off to the side during the violence.
a girl calls me. says, it was me talking, beckylane.
I say, oh yes. of course. I feel a tremendous familiarity with her
know I know her well but can't place her at all. she talks with
obvious thrill to see me. me feeling like teacher to her she anxious to show me two drawings. both done in pencil. before and
after. the drawings change before my eyes become clearer and
clearer they are indicative of severe abuse I know. I move closer
to get a better view a better understanding feel a large danger
behind me looming threatening warning me not to get too close
so close. then I know I won't be able to stand aside unnoticed.
I'll be forced by the group pressured to do their violence.

dec 28 / 91

I'm so scared. just trying to keep myself alive. doing all
this incredible personal work and doing grad work too.
trying to subvert the value of something I myself value
tremendously: literature. but what academe has done to it
with it to the study of it. preparation for publication for
the study of critics of academics not poets or novelists or
teaching?

Advice will be given to you
well worth following.

One of these people suffered years of torture by a group of rural
farmers. One suffered years of torture by a group of frenzied sex
addicts and pornographers, one by a satanic cult, and one by a
professional doctors' group.

— Shirley Turcotte [a]

dec 28 / 91

how to keep the past and present separate. keep having flashes
until they become memories.
where does all the wax go when it doesn't drip down the sides?

At lunch with a group of feminist scholars in a prairie city,
I am told that sexual abuse and incest are inappropriate topics
of conversation.

— Janice Williamson

dec 28 / 91
looking up at the baby. she's dying she's going to die.
moving like crying but I can't hear her. it's too loud.
the girl in the dream is me. my little girl knows me and
trusts me. she's trying to show me my past.
I won't be an individual. I'll have to do their violence.
I didn't choose to go there as a child. I'm now choosing
to go back. I can't stand aside and watch now any more
than I could then.
I am a pacifist. I have an intense aversion to violence.
I must stand inside and protect my frightened child.
she needs me.
I can't remember the drawing in my dream. and right now,
I can't remember what happened with the baby. I know
she's the same baby I was forced to pack with potatoes.
I need to remember so I can live.

dec 29 / 91
I'm so frustrated. wanting to perceive myself from a positive
perspective. so fucking hard.

a machine. press this button for love. feel it? press this button for
compassion. shame: no button required.
I can't do this, margaret. I'm fooling myself. I'm not good
enough. I don't deserve it. I'll see. my life will fall apart. I'm
filth. can't you tell? you don't share with me. self-disclosure you
call it. you say you share more with all your other clients. why?
you'll have to think about it, you say. have you thought about it?
it's because I'm slime. a fuck. a cunt. it shows through no matter
what I do. the more I try the more it will show through.
I'm so tired. so tired of the struggle.

READERS: With regards to journal entries and narration about
the therapy process, we would like you to include some mention
of difficulties in the therapeutic relationship, so it rings more true.
This is not asking you to slam your therapist, but for the benefit
of presenting a more accurate picture there should be some acknowledgement of difficulties between you.

dec 29 / 91
read through diary no. 1 from more than three years ago.
wow. speechless. could I doubt myself after that? yes, of course I
could I'm so good at self-doubt. I have come have I come a long
way. not a hope I could do what I'm doing now, then. gives me
hope. I know I can do it.

yesterday gregory said, you know mom, things are better at home than they've ever been. I like the way you've raised me and I appreciate the respect you give me. you've come so far away from the way your family is, mom. you deserve a lot of credit. hold those thoughts, beckylane.

I'm so fragile. my bones can break, my skin exposed to the cold. tiny tiny me. growing. the wise wise parrot I know many languages many moods I am old.

dec 30 / 91
saw margaret. talked, almost fluidly, finally. almost three years. I feel shame for my lack of trust and also not. the lack of trust (more than anything) comes with being a survivor of ritual abuse. I was programmed not to trust.
she had some really positive comments. that I do so much even while working on such difficult personal issues. successful in school and with my kids. she said she had this image of me in a dark tunnel. puts down her pencil and puts her hands out in front of her like diving only straight ahead. she said it's like you push ahead, push it to the sides and then to the back all the way back and behind you. points her two thumbs back.

jan 01 / 92

1992. how do you do? never thought I'd live so long.
inventory. how do I feel? quiet. two thumbs back. taking the time
it takes. to accept and believe and claim my past is so important
to my present and to my future. my kids' futures. I want to believe. this year, I know I'll believe.
I'm afraid to label my dad as the monster who tortured me during
my childhood. I wasn't separate from him and I'd therefore be a
monster myself. I've often thought of myself as a monster. when
someone disliked me I thought it must be my fault.
I choose not to be a member of an abusive family. beckylane
cleaning-up-the-name-

                              I choose not to be a member of
an alcoholic and drug-abusive family.

                              I choose to believe my
memories. I will. two thumbs back.

A FRIEND OF A FRIEND: Your father must have suffered
tremendously as a child.
ME: Yes, I'm sure he did. But it absolves him of nothing.
I've never had the urge to abuse/rape/torture my kids.

jan 01 / 92

it's a long journey, beckylane. pack a good lunch. wear
comfortable durable footwear. and take your shoes off in the
warm soft sand. sit in the sun for a while. love yourself.
you're worth it.

jan 02 / 92

two thumbs back. believe it, beckylane. my instinct/instant can
be so negative toward myself. you will fail, beckylane. you're a
fake. full of hot air. such repulsive stuff. it's so hard to love
myself first instinct/instant. I just don't. oh, how I want to. to
view myself unencumbered, positive first.
I am a nice person. n i c e. direct but not aggressive,
margaret once said. for me, the niceties of
education/station/class/wealth/profession mean very little
as silent proper power protection-barriers. ideological
blablabla boundaries social skills. break down the dams see
they're not beavers they're not bears the kind of abuse I
suffered nullifies all pretty paper-talk. it crosses over to
all segments — church/law/education/medicine/psychology/
science. no one is safe. anyone could be one of them.

I'm tired of everything. feeling okay shitty okay shitty shitty
okay. one face I wear one wears me out. I look into the mirror
what do I see? me. flying. still no body.

You are about to make a most
valuable discovery.

jan 04 / 92
a break in the line. gregory left this morning to go to school.
my heart heavy my love for him profound. a natural, extremely
difficult moment. my boychild is ready to fly.

jan 05 / 92
I looked at photographs of my parents yesterday. felt hatred for
my mother. nothing for my father. nothing.

jan 06 / 92
saw margaret today. how do I feel? sad. tired. like I want to quit.
everything. therapy school life.
talked about two confusing dreams recurring. about the
photographs. said I felt hatred for my mother. margaret said, you
shouldn't have to feel that way about your mother. I said, what
way? she said, you shouldn't have to feel hate for your mother.
my mother beat me kicked me violated me, violently, with
douches and enemas until I bled treated me like some kind of
poisonous snake.

A DREAM: large bathrooms. blood-soaked clothes.
toilets overflowing with waste. toilets that are
holes in the floor. crowded. no privacy. no place
to go to the bathroom. blood-soaked panties.
redblood fresh red red dripping wet.

A DREAM: running up a hill. snow. white white. stop right
at the edge where the snow is cliff down down far down
carefully cut squared-off snow cliffs.

she lines us up for enemas   some sit on buckets   soap
and water enemas   deworming
                    I look for the worms
                    never see any

                                            my mommy
is born bad   me too   some girls are just born that way

                                            my mommy
says we were born for it   her fault my fault god curses
our bodies
                    your body is evil
                    your body is filth
                                            my mommy
screaming at a monster
                         me

jan 06 / 92
she was afraid of many things. birds snakes escalators. me.
not all little girls. me. I was a little little little girl and my mommy
was afraid of me. called me evil. said she wished I was dead.
she was badly abused herself.
so was my dad.
if I shouldn't have to feel that way about my mom, then I
shouldn't have to feel that way about my dad. I want to hate him.
I want to experience him as separate from me and I want to
believe my past and I want to hate that asshole.
I didn't beat my kids kick force enemas douches hate reject wish
them dead

the other she does with only me
                              the same thing she uses for
deworming   same one   fills it with something and
                       forces the black stick into my peepee
                         push   squeeze
                         push   squeeze
                                   until liquid and
blood and blood gushes down my legs
                                   you are a dirty evil child
                                   this is your dirty evil place
                                             the cunt
                                   your cunt is filthy
                                   your cunt is filthy
                       stop your bitching or I'll never stop
                                   stop your crying
                                   shut your mouth
                                        bitch

jan o6 / 92

when I was a child, I could never hate my mother. I tried so hard
oh so hard to win her love. but she wouldn't/couldn't/didn't.
she hated me more I couldn't do anything right. the only time
was when I was seven after the farm after the dead baby. then
when I came back from summer vacation the same year and there
was a letter she'd printed to me. I knew she wrote handwriting.
printing was so hard (for me) and as hard for her (I thought).
writing was fast and easy, but not printing. and there was money
in it in the letter and my parents so poor. I read and read and
read the letter. believed my mom really she really loves me she
says so right here. the words I can read them look beckylane
look. but it got the same again. worse. sometimes my mom acted
like I wasn't even in the room. if I spoke to her she would just
move through the air as if she'd heard and seen nothing. no one.
she didn't even look or talk or anything. to me. she would talk to
whoever else was in the room and make me invisible. I felt so
bad. I must be bad. thought about what I did I do why does she
treat me this way?

                                        I don't cry
                                she hears her own yell
                                she sees me the child

                    six
            stone
                                                she cleans me up
                        blood
                pee
                                            she cleans the floor
                                                    dresses me
                                        she wants to give me food

        no mommy
            not food
                    can't talk   want to go outside
                                the day in the dirt I don't cry
                                she tries to make me but I don't

hurts so much
the cool dirt feels good on my skin
the trees are my friends
            they will protect me
            they will make the noise go away
            their voices quiet   loud quiet
                                            my mommy hates me
            rocking
            me   my mommy hates me

BECKYLANE'S REPORT CARD, AGE 6: Beckylane is still slow to answer orally, but knows the work well. Her neatness is commendable. Beckylane has been promoted (with honours) to

A SCHOLAR: What strikes me about this piece is that you don't take enough credit for who you are who you've become the woman who survived all that and herself obviously became a good mother. This probably says more about me than about you because of my interest in mother-daughter relationships, but I would have liked to have seen more of you and your kids in here. I found myself connecting up that one incident with your mother, the one where she seems to realize there's something seriously wrong, the one where she reaches out to save you I guess (if you can call anything saving, in that world), the one where she bathes you or something. And then the one where your daughter says she feels safe when you hold her like that. I think it's important for other women, women who are abused themselves, to know it's possible, to know there's hope. The courage that it takes even to leave an abusive marriage! You don't even talk about that here. There's only one sentence about that.

things have changed quite dramatically with me in me in that I have accessed a power of choice. to choose whether or not to perceive myself as okay. now I can fight that familiar feeling even at its surface. it's a good feeling.

jan 06 / 92

I'm tired. I have to hate my mother in order to hate my father. my mother acted like I was invisible after the episode when I was seven. she refused to love me again. and my father refused to hate me. I need to separate from my father and I need to bond with my mother. intellectually, I can imagine this. emotionally, however, all I can remember is my pain.

I'm struggling to survive. I have a deep deep need to destroy myself. I have rejected the negativity that was superimposed onto me. that I'm innately evil. that I'm cursed. that there's nothing I can do about it because I was born that way. for whatever reason. no reason. I want to die. it would be so much easier than life. my life.

jan 07 / 92

I'm struggling to believe. to have memory wiped out. erased. gone. then to have these images come from inside. pictures as clear as dreams. when I remembered something in the past, I remembered the picture, the feelings, I put myself there again. but these memories put themselves here. my eyes inside my eyes of my past. I see out my eyes again. not like dreams where sometimes I see out my eyes and sometimes I see my whole self. not like voluntary memories where I see out my eyes but also feel with my body. I can't put myself there until I believe. fully. with my body all of me. right now, I talk like I believe. I talk about that past as mine. the words come out and go back in through my own ears. but I don't really believe my own talk. even though

what I say is original and spontaneous and too real and detailed
to be believed in fiction, I don't really believe.
I remember reading somewhere that people with returning
memories like mine more often than not find it difficult to believe
themselves. and that ritually abused people who have repressed
the abuse may be the last to believe; after their counsellors,
families, friends know or believe their experiences. right now,
it helps to know is all.

the complexities, from my perspective, are too numerous and
inaccessible to verbalize and sometimes even to think into
thought. what I want and what I need and what I actually get
are ever-changing and incongruous.

the pain the suffering the struggle toward a wholeness that was
denied me in childhood. stripped of positive. the positive peeled
from the air around me now and way back then when I left it
here and there. the gatherer. the gardener. the healer.

A SCHOLAR: You know, once this text is published, once it's out there, you will have to defend it during interviews. You'll be asked to explain what makes this piece different. What makes it worth reading? It's been done before, they'll say. How will you deal with that psychologically? Will you even be able to handle that kind of criticism?

ME: I don't understand your questions. This is not intended as "entertainment." It's a way of reaching out to other people who were abused as children with a hope of helping them through the pain of their own healing. It's a way of reaching those people who were not abused themselves with a hope of helping them to understand some of its implications. I don't understand your point. Are you suggesting that because one incest testimony has been written, any other is redundant unless it reveals a more sensational "plot-line" or a more clever form of articulation? Heard one incest story, heard them all: is that it?

I've been "criticized" by the experts. I'm not intimidated by possible difficult questions during possible interviewing processes, if that's what you mean. My experiences have not made me into a delicate and emotionally fragile person who will fall to pieces under pressure.

Incest speaks to first-hand experience

Ritual abuse speaks to first-hand experience

Writing speaks

Reading listens and hears

jan 08 / 92

now I know why I have such limited movement in my arms.
hanging hanging by my wrists. why I was so terrified of my
womanness terrified of those boxes of menstrual pads used
tampons, that helped, so happy at twenty-six a hysterectomy
endometriosis we're so sorry three specialists tests and tests
you'll need a hysterectomy. yes!
ashamed of my glee. always so much trouble with digestion can't
eat much have to eat so slowly so much diarrhea poor appetite
smell of meat makes me feel sick. raw red meat. broken chicken
bones hey just keep a grip beckylane it's just a broken chicken
bone.
so many bladder infections kidney infections when I was young.
slow down, beckylane. maybe some academic reading will be a
good change.

All the troubles you have
will pass away very quickly.

jan 08 / 92

now read and read the articles again. ritual abuse. it's okay,
beckylane. memories can't kill. it's important to remember,
more important than not. it hurts so much. nonsense dreams.
needing so much privacy now in the bathroom in my bedroom.
had to be examined by a physician at a blood donor clinic. it's

okay beckylane she's just a young woman cold hands hurry hurry
creepy don't want my body touched. she senses my apprehension.
are you okay she asks. me, yes, I'm okay. but I'm not.
going back going back getting myself ready to remember more
and more detail.

jan 09 / 92
all the fears I worked to overcome worked so hard to overcome I
don't want them back. fear of water bugs blood sleeping in a car
outhouses alcohol drugs doctors authorities sharp knives rotting
potatoes night silence sound sleep touch.
all these I worked so hard. water and bugs and blood the hardest.
did it, though. desensitize.
pig farms. barns. cement floors. it got easier and easier.
I don't want these fears back.
                        I don't have to have them back.
just understand where they came from is all. go back using the
skills I've learned, naturally. go back in strength not horror.
still terrified of sound sleep and pig farms.

jan 09 / 92
same day feeling shitty. keep writing, beckylane.
write it out.   why?
because you always feel better when you write it out.
ya, talking to myself in the second person. really with it.

---

whatever gets me through. lived it all once now I have to do
it all over again. right now it feels endless. I wish I'd
remembered all along then at least I wouldn't have this
struggle so much doubt. so much.

put the pieces together.

how?   believe.

how?

patience.

if I had one shred, one real feel/know connection. the image.
not the body. my body I have no body. I want my body back.

jan 10 / 92
had a flash image memory before going to sleep last night a girl
curly brown hair agony on her face on a bed being raped.
this is so hard. so many feelings knowing how she felt.
I'm going through such a hard time. important, I know, to try to
keep some kind of perspective. yesterday at school I felt so good.
home.
I can do this. if I couldn't do it I wouldn't be doing it. as simple
as that.

BECKYLANE'S SISTER: Hey, Dad helps us out whenever he
can. He bakes bread. He always gives us one or two loaves, you
know? Never forgets anyone's birthday, which is more than I
can say for you. We get by. So I treat myself to a little cheap

wine every once in a while. So I spank my kids every once in
a while. How else would I get them to do what they're told?
A little discipline never hurt anyone. At least I don't work. At
least I'm here for my kids. Not like you, out there doing who
knows what wasting your life away at university. You must really
think you're something, eh? Some hotshot. I wish my life was as
easy as yours.

jan 13 / 92
finally feeling better. finally. having some of my power back,
and the bonus is, it's clearer and stronger. one thing for sure:
I'm completing this trip because I'm sure as hell not going to
deliberately put myself on this plane ride again. it's just too
damned treacherous and I don't even have a license. my life. shit.
realize I still have a major fear (probably many). vomit. one I've
never overcome. you mess it, cunt, you eat it. shit.

You have a wise spirit, an advanced intellect
and faith in human nature.

AN ADULT SURVIVOR OF RITUAL ABUSE: Now this abuse
occurs in the name of God the Father. You see, we're told that
we won't burn in Hell like everybody else after the day of God's

judgment. God the Father, mind. God the Son and God the Holy
Spirit'll be there too, along with their one hundred and forty-four
thousand "which were redeemed from the earth. These are they
which were not defiled with women" (*Rev. 14.3,4*). Hey gang,
these are they which are not *born* from women. So who're they
born from? Well, that's one of the Great Mysteries. The rest of
us billions who're born from women belong to Satan, they tell us.
But if you're in the cult, you won't be burning like those other
suckers. You'll be in Hell all right, but you'll be working for the
Big Cheese and you won't be suffering.
What a load of human waste after all is what I think. And I
would know. I know what it tastes like what it feels like to
breathe it. To be immersed in it, for hours. To have it in my
nostrils in my ears my hair my throat in my

                                               teeth.
We've *got* to stop this! We're all responsible, I tell you.
As long as you're one of the ones who's ho-hum ho-hum trying
to decide whether or not ritual abuse really *exists*, another
child is murdered. Raped. Tortured. Beaten.

        Another child is screaming for *your* help!

on the edge. on the edge. in control and on the verge of tears.
knowing I'll be okay. not cluttered or confused. but definitely
on the edge.

---

jan 27 / 92
letters that don't want to fit themselves into words.

jan 29 / 92
one face I wear one wears me out.
ted says, people are going to want you to change this to that
about your writing. me too. but I think it's my maleness I think
you should just keep on doing what you do. push it further.

jan 30 / 92
denial. the implications of my past overwhelming to me.
should I take a break from all of this? memory images
wherever I go. can I?
feeling so alone.
feeling close to breaking to burnout.
silent to my talking in my diary. wanting success. don't let
the bastards grind you down feeling like I'm caught inside a
combine hovering until I can reassemble all the bleeding parts
of my own body.

jan 31 / 92

the past wanting to destroy me before I can destroy what it has
not done to me. it has not destroyed me.

I have a very strong personal and professional support system.
sally always steady support loving kind you can do it beckylane
you're doing it keep going just keep going. arel. wilhelmina.
aladin. jim. others all around. gregory. samantha. wayne. my
mind rushes into crossed/webbed labyrinths of self-loathing that
I want to soothe into love. I'm tired of the familiar way of self-
loathing. that I deserve only to suffer and to fail. I need to gather
and weave in silky love affirmation.

gather your strength, woman. I'm worth it
to me to my kids my friends.

the memories that come, come
for me. so as not to frighten me into madness. memories of
my father fuzzy and disguised. they have to be. I will
survive this horror. I am meant to. all of these avenues of
success are gifts.

my past is mine
my present is mine too

feb 01 / 92

six o'clock. all the troubles you have will pass away very quickly.
my message in a fortune cookie.

I am beginning to believe.

10 Reasons Why I Would Falsely Accuse My Parents of Incest or
Ritual Abuse

> 9. I wanted to be different, special and get
>   lots of attention by breaking down and
>   becoming incapable of supporting or
>   taking care of myself.
>
> — Jezanna Rainforest

feb 02 / 92
helped arel and aladin birth their baby. monique. such a joy
words can't do my awe my love. lucky me.

———

Ritual abuse is the breaking down of a person — for example, sexually and mentally — by an organized or semi-organized group in a repetitive fashion over time. This abuse can be perpetrated within a range of institutional settings, including religious settings residential schools, business settings, hospitals, the military, penal systems or commuity-based settings, just to name a few. It can be people involved in child pornography rings or members within an extended family. There is often a small group hiding within the fabric of a larger group, stealing the resources and networking capacity of the larger group to do their dirty business and protecting themselves under the reputation of the larger group. They can be highly sophisticated, using advanced brainwashing techniques, or crude and unsophisticated, using random acts of brainwashing.

— Shirley Turcotte [b]

feb 03 / 92
how can I not believe my past? so alone. if this is not my past I'm remembering, what is my past? what fills in the gaps?

so many gaps

so

feb 03 / 92
I am beginning to believe.

Even so, the reaction to the "recovered memory" phenomenon
has risen to the point last year where a formal organization — the
False Memory Syndrome Foundation — appeared in Phila-
delphia, and it has since spawned a branch in Canada. The False
Memory Syndrome Foundation argues that repression is bunk. Its
members insist that any genuine memory of a deeply traumatic
experience would be too vivid to be repressed. One major factor
that may skew the accuracy of what's being recalled is expecta-
tion. The mind fills in any blanks or gaps . . .

— Kirk Makin [b]

1. Problems associated
with sexual behaviour and beliefs:
states that sharp objects
were inserted in his/her private areas
states (s)he
witnessed sex acts between adults, adults and children,
adults or children and animals

in any gaps or blanks

———

                              5. Problems associated
with death:
                fears (s)he will die on her/his sixth birthday
        in any blanks or gaps
                              9. Emotional problems (including
speech, sleep, learning problems):
                              11. Problems associated
with play and peer relations:
                        acts out death, mutilation,
cannibalism, and burial themes by pretending to kill play
figures, taking out eyes,

                in any
                        gaps
                                or

                                        talks
about animals, babies, human beings confined, hurt, killed,
mutilated, eaten,

        gaps

or dialogue it anticipates would have been logical under
— Kirk Makin [b]

Your road will be made smooth for you
by good friends.

feb 03 / 92
this morning samantha said, it's so nice to know that
there's new life.
I have the opportunity to know new life. I fight it like
it's a demon. it's my past I'm fighting. furiously.

feb 04 / 92
love is its own reality. smells yellow mauve pale green.
watercolours. many things exist we have no words for no place
in a book in the air where words move out against the sky.
when I was a child I dreamed words, letters, black and illegible,
against the blue. they frightened me. they covered large areas
black marks everywhere but not in the air around me. I thought
the sky was far away and placed there flat and blue against a wall
of glass.

feb 06 / 92
my dad was an asshole. big time. it's all here for me. see? see?
look and see me crying crying so many tears rush a river all my
water out. rock me sing me into me.
so alone.
don't push so hard. let it out slowly.
I have to love myself through this. not hate, love.

READERS: Someone commented on repetitive language on
the theme of "loving yourself is all you need for recovery."
While understanding that self-love is a crucial component,
and it certainly may be the major objective in therapy, that
language can signify a totally apolitical stance — like the only
thing that needs to change is you, not the society that tolerates
victimization of women and children and allows ritual abuse
to continue without punishment.

feb 07 / 92
maybe it's time for a break.
I don't know. I think, if I take a break I've failed. if I take
a break I won't go back.
concentrate on belief, then. like now.

misunderstood abused so badly. what is love anyway? I know
I love my kids. deep deep waterwarm. I know they love me like
kids can love their mothers must. my friends. they say I help they
help me too but give myself? open myself apart to love? here.
love me. I've never done it, it's not been done to me. there's
some way I've never been loved it's medicine it's healing it's by
prescription only in the therapist's room the bottle where the
drug confines itself.

feb 08 / 92
during my childhood I was so abused misunderstood.
I know I'm not a child now but emotionally, in therapy and out,
I still believe (beginning to not) that I am evil.
I know I'm not and I feel I am.
redoing. relearning. rebecoming.

feb 09 / 92
my difference was not valued by those others, my parents. it was,
in fact, feared and detested and shunned and denied and beaten
raped shattered. children of alcoholics feel different from other
people. I know that. but I feel different in a different way, I think.
my friends tell me I'm different.

WILHELMINA: Well you're certainly different from anyone I've ever met. I mean, I know quite a few older people and you are the only one, bar none, who doesn't try to use your age as a form of power, who doesn't talk down to me from your superior position of wisdom and experience. You consistently treat me like an equal.

feb 10 / 92
I see it in my mothering. I see it everywhere. but I can't accept my positive difference because I was not accepted as positive.

the devil's cunt

cursed

these are the things I internalized.

SALLY: Just look at your writing. It's so psychologically insightful.

feb 10 / 92

my mother's fear of me. different from her fear of birds or
snakes or cats or escalators because it was me specifically, not
kids generally or little girls, but me.
my mother was sensitive and intuitive and powerful in my family.
she was respected valued for the intuitive parts of herself. her
feelings about others were adopted by everyone inside and many
outside the family. and she feared me distrusted me hated me
loved me. wanted me dead invisible.

                                             disappeared me
she destroyed my childhood photographs. all of them except
the family portrait when I was five. there are pictures of
my siblings baby pictures toddler pictures childhood
pictures. but not me.

                           I never had a childhood birthday
party. the others did oh yes they did but I was better dead
she said. she made me make the cake decorate too because I
was best at that kind of

                              convinced, even me, that I didn't deserve
to be loved and nurtured. I was not okay. I was evil.
powerful and evil.

                                        two
            under the kitchen table
                                in the dark
scared
                                        alone

there is something bad going on in my room
I'm afraid to go back there
I feel the bigness of the house
I want it to be small
                    small like here   under the table
    I'm not allowed here   daddy says   pokes me with the
broom stick   jabs   it's safe here though   I know

                    it's our house   grampa's house
                                                    so big
my old room's down   on the down floor   at the back
I go in here   I like it here   it feels good   smells good
                    sleeping
                            I wake up
mommy's here too   hi mommy

REMARKABLY, about one in five cases of abuse recalled later in life feature satanism

— Kirk Makin [b]

Remarkable.   *a.* 1604. Worth notice, exceptional; striking, conspicuous

— *Oxford Dictionary*

[People] with severe abuse histories can also teach a great deal about aspects of the interconnection of mind and body as well as the extremes of human capability. For example, most [people] with such backgrounds report various types of special abilities from ESP to the ability to heal rapidly from injuries. Our understanding of these areas is not even in its infancy. It clearly would be very valuable to understand and perhaps learn possible applications for [these] process[es] in the general population.

— David K. Sakheim and Susan E. Devine

mommy's so mad
hitting   hitting

sneaky little bitch always spying
evil eye   you've got the evil eye

you know too much go away
I wish you'd never been born

you should've died when I was in the car accident
I wanted you to die   I hate you

you caused it   the accident   willed it with your evil
hitting   hitting   kicking

everyone says it   you should be dead   you know too much
go away   go away   get

It is important to connect ritual abuse to all of the forms of violence that surround us. In that context, it becomes less and less possible to disbelieve. Ritual abuse is on a continuum of violence, and on that continuum there are many comparable crimes. For instance, those committed in Nazi concentration camps or by the Ku Klux Klan; or the murder, sadism and ritualized torture that routinely go on in wars. And, to bring the issue back to the homefront, the terrorization of children through repeated family violence.

— Gail Fisher-Taylor

feb 11 / 92

you've worked so hard. like cindy says, you've done it all on your own. no more self-hate self-doubt. you can do it just look at what you've done already. simply amazing, woman. cheer up, woman. you're reading poetry next week. presenting a paper next month. you *are* succeeding. the self-doubt will come and go.

feb 15 / 92

I really am feeling better. still.

feb 19 / 92

each time I come through one of those great gaping holes in the air, I feel so much better. this time I want to stay here. to keep the anxious self-deprecatory pull to self-loathing out. stay strong. be strong.

secrets are bad   I know   my sisters have secrets
          don't tell mommy
          don't tell mommy
          shhhh   shhhh
          don't tell mommy

                    she screams and screams
how'd you get in here anyway if you tell anyone about this
I'll kill you I swear I'll kill you
             covered up in the bed   a big bump
    like daddy

I crawl fast very fast to underneath the table way back
under by where the cat goes   scared

                   she screams and screams
come out from there you little bitch

    hug the wall   me   hug   me
    hear my heart beat beat beat   hurts
           scared
           scared scared of mommy
bad girl   bad girl   shaking   cold
     sleeping

how could my father live and function in the world? smile?
laugh? succeed at work? read the paper? be a pro-lifer? go to
church? pray? believe in himself as a good person?

If we do not change our direction we are likely
to end up where we are headed.

feb 26 / 92
do I even have anything to say? sitting on this bench in the sun.
warm and comforting and poison now. who's responsible?
who's not? only children.

Because society tends to doubt stories of ritual abuse, this attitude
carries over into the court system.

— Elizabeth S. Rose

feb 27 / 92
valuing myself will take a long long time. the mindless work of a
child. an unconscious process forced into consciousness.

mar 02 / 92
saw margaret this morning as the hard gets easier, relatively
speaking. started stopped diverted started again to tell her some
of my fears. consumed with shame. said, I have worked through
some of these fears very creatively yet I feel shame. it doesn't
make sense. she says, yes it does. that the root is in shame so it's
the shame that resurfaces. I think, of course. after about an hour
this morning, I no longer felt shame. usually it takes days

10 Reasons Why I Would Falsely Accuse My Parents of Incest or
Ritual Abuse

> 3. I decided, for a change of pace, to begin
>   experiencing bouts of intense suicidality.
> 4. I wanted to wake up in the middle of the
>   night screaming in terror and unable to
>   breathe, re-experiencing over and over
>   the times I was "not" raped as a child.
> 5. I wanted [to] experience, first-hand, what
>   a mental institution or prison was like.
>   — Jezanna Rainforest

mar 04 / 92

something good going on here. talked to arel today. I can't
believe what you've been through how exceptional your kids
are, she says. one day, and I think it's soon, you're going to
realize how gifted you are. I can't wait, she says. me: I don't
know if that will happen but something good is going on here.
in here in me.

mar 17 / 92
scared.
sounds childlike.
yes. I am not a child. I have children and I am almost forty.
at some time I won't feel afraid. but not yet. when I can embrace
myself my past I'll feel better.
my father. that old goofy-looking man without a shred of
self-confidence. the monster washed away completely. what will
happen at the shore?
he'll wash up in all his bald ugliness.
my fears my life my dreams tell me, yes.
I want to succeed to believe my own write to mix the right the
left in language.
each morning I wake up hating myself. hate in process. didn't
even know until I started loving myself.
I feel content. for the first time in my life I feel content with
belief and acceptance. a fluid inside in which I know I glow.
for real.

lawyers I've talked to say that my account in itself should be "proof" enough. that I should publish the name of the law firm that represented my father so that victims of abuse know where *not* to go for legal representation. even if I had the courage or the cash to proceed with criminal charges, I probably wouldn't succeed until the court of appeal level, they tell me. it would be a long and difficult process and I would be subjected to intense revictimization throughout. the courts would assume that either I am lying or my father is. we would be "equally" interrogated. this is *so* serious. people don't want to hear it because it is *so* far beyond what we expect or want people who sit next to us in restaurants and in churches and at work to be capable of. and people have been desensitized to violence and murder by the media and by television. murder is fun. like football or boxing. it's a stress release. everyone knows it's not real, after all. but think of the *real* children, I say. just think of the children and only of the children. the ones who die and will continue to die for as long as people continue to deny; think of the ones who will not die, but like me, will carry this with them and will be afraid to tell afraid of being murdered themselves.

A CHILD SURVIVOR: Maybe fear makes people disbelieve. I can only say what happened and hope you'll listen. Just be me for a while — you should have lived through what I did — just be my cousins still going through it. If you won't listen then there's nothing left.

mar 21 / 92
my dad was a binary. love or hate. no middle, no balance. me too.
I could love or hate myself. hate made more sense.

Your business superiors have you definitely
in mind for a promotion.

Your enterprise will
bring great profit.

mar 25 / 92
when I come close to belief to believing what my dad did to me
subjected me to I become small small fetal disappear into hate
self-hate shame on you shame.

mar 29 / 92
everything on the outside says my past exists. or could exist.
everything on my inside says it did.
break through the air, beckylane.
what am I afraid of?
the old definition. that the old definition will seep through and
define me. that it's true.

I am the devil's child
I tried to kill my mommy before I was born

she says so she tells everyone watch out for that one not of this world
that one tried to kill me before she was born that one eight-and-a-half
months pregnant and she tried to kill me in a car accident she caused
it that one willed it with her evil see she has a third eye that one the
evil eye

Society has got to stop denying. Technologically we've advanced to a great degree and people think that means the human animal has advanced to that same degree. But that isn't true. We're the same basic animal we've always been. If people can imagine these things going on four and five hundred years ago, then they have to start believing that they are happening today. It's time for people to get out of the denial stage so we can stop it.

— Sandi Gallant

BECKYLANE'S BROTHER: Ah, you just think you're so damned smart, don't ya? Always trying to impress people with your logical book-talk. Little Miss Smart-Ass. Mom was right about you. She told me many times to stay away from you.
Now I finally know what she was talking about, eh? Mom was a saint. A saint, ya hear? There isn't a day in my life that I don't think of her. And I won't hear a bad word spoken about her, hear? Dad's no saint, but what the hell. What the hell, eh? Those were the times, my dear. Everyone hit their kids in those days.

I am the oldest of three sons born to an upper-middle-class
family. We lived on a gentleman's farm with animals to care for,
a beautiful southern colonial home
                              my father was extremely handsome
                    mother unbelievably beautiful
                                                              — Dan

apr 03/92
what to say? I feel so mixed up inside I want it to stop and not.
keep moving. it's so difficult to word out this slowly as slowly as
writing. probably better this way. so confused him my dad where
does he fit resistance stronger than desire.
                                        a huge gap a
                                              silence
                                    wanting to speak
                                    what does it mean?
it's not linear back and forth from small to bigger small to bigger
how to coax the words out. come on out, words. come on out.
they're so far away in the sky. pull them down fly up and get
them I have all these pieces what do they mean?
calm stay calm no I want to burst out of this cocoon this
mechanical calm.
calm is good but maybe not right now frustrated and ready to
burst. break out

apr 03 / 92

I felt lucky after my dad started raping me at home. I
didn't know why didn't know I had a past eating vomit
innards animals babies pee shit or torture pain pain oh the
pain or
I don't want to let go of the lucky feeling because then
I'll have to go back there

        back and forth back and forth stay away

              from the agony the fast fast

    unrealness

I don't want to and I want to. the past the present tugging at the
past. I want to put all the feelings together. to allow them to mix.
I handled this. I handled this.
one compartment another.
then I don't want to feed myself. I *need* food. I want to take care
of myself on the inside. don't tell don't tell. you may not eat.

what am I eating?

eat it, cunt

A READER (who is aware of a sibling's experiences of ritual abuse but has no personal memory of same): Well, you can't blame people for not wanting to hear this.

ME: Can't blame people? What's "blame"? How does it fit? All they have to do is have their ears assaulted by words, their psyches assaulted by images, their feelings threatened. I, on the other hand, had to live it. I didn't ask for it I didn't do it and neither did all the other children who were forced into it. This has to be spoken. To be heard. Without the shame/blame being placed with those who are breaking the silence. Consider the audience? Be sensitive to their need for silence? Temper the blow? I don't think so. The impact of words is only the

apr 03 / 92
I come up from inside myself
        big and mean
           love on the outside
        hate inside

                         I want the outside in the inside
                                     out

get it out, beckylane.
mechanically I know how to take care of myself but what do I want? I want to believe. to put all the pieces together and believe. believe what?
all of it. I have these vivid images I refuse to call memory. what are they if they're not memory?

---

re-member.
you perceive your father as, literally, fragmented, says margaret.

                    waiting
            they're waiting
                the buds are waiting
                            waiting for what
        the right combination
        of light and air
        of water and love
                        waiting for the right moment
what's in there that wants to come out?
put all the pieces together.
how?
with love?
ah shit, I don't know.
I have a feeling inside an urgency I'm almost there.
where?
hell if I know. almost there.
talk. I want to talk. I want to answer questions. I want to
question answers.
                        other
            the silenced other
            my silenced other
                    my otherness from him
                    I hate myself my him
            my dad is in me I want him

                                        out

apr 04 / 92
what does that mean, my dad is in me.
it means I haven't separated from him. I want to protect
him.
from what?
from me.
say what?
I am the devil's cunt. if I wasn't the devil's cunt my dad
wouldn't have done all those things to me.
it's my fault. it's all my fault.
I was a child
no.
they convinced me. I was not a child but using a child's
body to do satan's work.
I can't separate myself out enough from my dad to
to what?
to realize that they must have said the same or similar things to
the other children.

apr 05 / 92
try to do this without smashing into thousands of small sharp
pieces. who will pick up the pieces for me? if I pick them up
I'll do it recklessly self-hate no I want to die I deserve to die.
die, cunt.
put gloves on. get a plastic bucket and put the pieces in
the bucket.
take care of yourself.

I'm so tired of taking care of myself I want someone to read me to anticipate my needs to take the risk and reach out. yet I know it's up to me. there's no one who can do it except for me.
a l o n e
but I'm not alone. I'm not alone. I'm the one who has to realize that.
forgetting the past comes back in memory it comes back so compressed. clear compressed.
only I can know how messed up I am. if I let go of the control, I'd go mad. let go slowly. fastslow.

The reasons the connections don't always seem to fit together is because my arms don't have the same experience my mouth had, and my eyes didn't feel what my stomach felt. I have felt like I was fractured into so many pieces, but it was the different parts of me remembering. I had to fracture that way. You see, "me" could not look after it all at once!

— Michelle Smith

apr 06 / 92

one day at a time. I understand as much as this: I'm afraid to go
beyond no feeling for my dad because I am afraid to remember
the ritual abuse. the abuse of me. the way I felt and the way I feel
or what that feeling is in me now. it's there.

it's still there the belief that I am a vehicle for satan. that it's my
fault. that my dad is okay and I'm not. that he did the best he
could with what he had to work with.

present tense.

if I heard someone else say this, how would I feel?

exasperated.

incredulous.

frustrated.

empathetic.

intellectually, I know

my dad is not okay and I am.

I guess then I'd believe someone else before I'd believe
myself?

apr 06 / 92
why is the feeling of 'my fault' still in me?
such an assault on the senses on the sense of right and wrong on
the sense of self. bashed and bruised. it must be true. I must be
the devil's child what else could I be?
these pieces.

                              it answered the question, why?

You'll never step on anyone's toes if you just
put yourself in their shoes.

———

A DREAM: four days running recurring. eyes closed but able
to see to drive even. trying to open my eyes. I can't see my eyes
won't open. I can't open them. yet I can and indeed am seeing.

apr 07 / 92
I can't open my eyes there. they're almost open.
here. two worlds. past and present. clash.

I could shut my eyes but my body could see what was happening.
— Michelle Smith

apr 08 / 92
what am I scared of?
I want to say, love.
say what?
scared of love? what does it mean? scared of love.
        I can see a glass door/wall between me and
        my feelings back then.
        what's behind the door?
        the ritual abuse.
so why love? why not, I'm scared of vulnerability. or rejection.
why love? and why scared? a little girl word.
love from me? from me. it's my love I'm afraid of.
why?
because I don't value my love for. primary love for. I tried to kill
my mom before I was born. I am the devil's cunt. my love is
poison.
        that's what's behind the glass door.
        a self-hatred so profound as to be out of

———

language. an indoctrination beyond
comprehension. I am not worth loving my
love is poison. I may seem nice but it's
the devil at work. I poison my parents
with my love. my love is poison. I will
not defile this earth with my love. it is
not love. I cannot love.
what about my kids my friends?
they're after the glass door.
they're not primary.
they are not in danger.

An introduction will alter
your plans.

apr 20 / 92
I am so closed. so holding myself in afraid to reach out across
the room even with my eyes.

———————

A DREAM: standing on a balcony many many houses built
on a steep mountainside. all uniform creamcolour. the balcony
wrought iron very black. bright sunlight stark shadows. a little
girl appears, throws her beach ball over the balcony, not
intentionally just throwing

                    dives through the holes in the wrought
iron to go after retrieve her ball she loves her ball its bright
colours. I watch, horrified. the child is gone. she must be dead,
I think. I couldn't save her it all happened so
but she lands somewhere below, in a swimming pool. she's fine.
the ball is the only thing that isn't dull muted colours sharpened
by sunlight. the ball the same bright colours as four dreams over
a period of four months same bright luminescent not florescent
hyper-primary yellow red blue violet brilliant alive warm pulse
all the colours are on the ball. all around. all attached. she is so
lucky but she is meant to be lucky. to live and have a story to tell.
she isn't afraid like me. she loves her ball too much to be afraid.

I had toys I loved my little stove and sink I loved it felt
love for it took it outside and played alone with it under
the neighbour's step in the dark in the sand cool sand sun
piercing through the slats in bright hot white lines
                              why do you play there my mother
asks you're so weird spook that's what you are don't play
there

apr 20 / 92

to love myself too much to be afraid. that's what I have to do.
all those colours, still in me. what do the colours represent?

apr 22 / 92

maybe the colours represent my optimism. kept me alive still
keep me alive.
the other day when samantha was feeling sick, I held her
silently. she said, I feel better, mom. I feel safe when you
hold me like this.

apr 23 / 92

dangerous liaisons. therapy. where does it begin end how far
do you go? where are the boundaries who decides? where is the
love? a slate, a blank page emptied of words in the air. the room
is full of words. the words are full of meaning. the meaning
is full of emotion. silence.
where does it fit? who is this woman? what is therapy? an
artificial environment designed to help the client to change her
behaviour through a cognitive relearning process.

Words, then, are not useful. Let us now inquire into their other quality, their positive quality, that is, their power to tell the truth.

— Virginia Woolf

GREGORY: How did you do it, Mom? I mean, really, with all
you're going through, with all you've gone through, how do you
do it? I had no idea how good I had it at home after you and Dad
got divorced. Always food in the fridge. Privacy. Respect, from
you and even from Samantha. I'm not saying that I want to move
back, I really am ready to do this on my own. But I sure
appreciate what you provided for me, Mom. You know, what I
really value about you as my mother is the respect you give me.
You've always taken my ideas seriously. You don't put pressure
on me to be someone I'm not. I like that. So many of my friends
have so many problems with their parents. Like Dad. He's behind
me 110%. He's 110% sure I'll fail. But every time I talk to you
I feel better. Better about myself, you know? Thanks, Mom.
Thanks.

apr 25 / 92
only at the end of each counselling session all the emotion in
through our bodies hold on hold. hold.
how can these emotions, so old, so raw, be translated into language? can you describe how you felt?
no. it's in my body.

apr 26 / 92
ebb and flow. I'm a sad sad woman right now. grief. no mommy.
no daddy. never.

apr 27 / 92
we've never shed a tear in this office, says margaret.

                                                  we.
do you weep? she asks when I tell her I allow myself to feel when
I'm alone.
                  yes, I say.
                              I've been forced to swallow the
excrement of horse cow sheep goat pig baby child women men
mine. I know what animal I smell. the blood the colour the
texture.
          I've been forced to swallow urine hot peed into my
face my eyes. I could make it taste like nothing.
                                                  I've
been forced to eat raw flesh sheep goat pig horse cow girl
babies girl children mine.
I could make it taste like nothing.
                                      I've been forced my head
my body forced under water under water until in the water I
am gone I want to die.
                          I've been lowered into
outhouses into faeces float float try to float in the dark
in the dark into graves dead bodies cold cold slime maggots
crawling gagging in the dark.
                              I've been hung on meat hooks.
always right wrist over left. right over left and under right over
left and under right over left and under I would chant over and
over and over a knot I learned in brownies. sometimes when I
fell asleep, hanging there, someone would pee in my face to
wake me up.

———

186

hard to hear?

hanging hanging

staring at my wrists my arms my hands. the detail of the hair in
my skin. such different skin than the skin I have now. each hair
with its little home.

hard to hear?

who'll read it?

STEPHANIE: If the lives of men who were in concentration
camps are respected and considered worth reading, a woman
who's been where you've been should be worth reading too.

apr 28 / 92
last year my dad sent me a card for my birthday. said it's about
time I came out of my 'self-imposed exile' and came back to the
family. glued something photocopied from a magazine on the
inside of the card. very bad poetry which I guess was meaningful

to him that if I love him let him know before death separates us and I can't let him know that I love him. I cut the card into very small pieces. put the pieces into an envelope. I'll mail them to him together with a letter, long before I die, and certainly before he dies. I want to do it this year. I hate my dad. he took away my childhood my dignity all of my self-esteem. I felt great when I cut the card. physical cut cut him up. hurt him. feel the strength of the blades. I hate that man. hate.

apr 30 / 92
I think I will feel stronger if I can talk about this with
other women who've been through this kind of debilitating
torture. I want to share. I am believing my own experiences
and I have a small understanding of how that kind of childhood
necessarily separates me from "the norm," just by virtue of the
kinds of skills I've had to develop in order to survive.
I'd like to reach a point where I feel the strength to reach out
and help other women other men children. I'd like to present
papers at conferences.
I need a community. I can remember how sure I was that sylvia
plath would have survived if only she'd had a community. she
became so isolated.

apr 30 / 92

my success has to come from the inside. like anjali today. her
success from the inside from her experiences as a woman from
scottish and south asian backgrounds. articulate. caring.
intelligent. doing what she loves to do.
today I'm both disappointed and proud of myself. the over-
powering feeling of inadequacy slowly dissipating into something
that belongs in my past. my clumsiness is becoming something
for me to value.

may 09 / 92

remembered in hypnosis. not what I expected not as bad in that I
thought I'd been involved in the baby's death and I guess I was in
that they killed her for/because of me.
I feel isolated and quiet but okay.
after the memory I was unable to open my eyes never wanted to
open them again.
almost a year to put together one memory. now, four days of
silence. the memory: I think I'll have a bath first.
had a bath. ate. the

hanging on a meat hook tied right wrist over left been there a long
long time no food no food hungry hungry no water keep falling asleep
that man keeps waking me up sometimes he pees in my face I can
make it taste like nothing
   the baby I can see the baby she's crying she's swollen

                purple

       close my eyes
        open your eyes cunt
   slaps me   open your eyes
        this is your lucky day

        I open my eyes

  lots of people come in they stand near the baby they
 sing they are singing they stand still

they roll up their sleeves someone comes in with a bucket
 they all start putting their hands in the bucket
            washing them
it's blood in the bucket people blood I can smell it

they pass the bucket to the man   he puts his hands in
rubs them   starts to rub the blood all over me   they're
all singing something I don't understand   he puts the
bucket over my head and pours it   slowly   into my hair
it's warm   it goes all over me down cold dripping
*   open your eyes*

*   I don't want to   it stings*

*   open them*

*   I do but I won't cry*
*   I am a big girl*

The idea of female wickedness and depravity was pounded into my head at the impressionable age of four. The life of a girl was an expendable commodity. In our cult, only female infants were sacrificed. Males were allowed to live. I was forced to watch as they killed my baby sister by decapitation in a ritual sacrifice. The death was never reported, because the birth had not been reported.

— Elizabeth S. Rose

may 14 / 92
having a difficult time coming to this process. not yet ready to write out the rest of the memory. it'll come.
I feel ready to move outward from myself and I'd like to start helping other women, not sure how yet.
I'd like maybe to be involved in workshops. to answer questions about and describe my process to help other counsellors in their work with ritually abused people.

may 15 / 92
I now believe that was my past.
margaret asked, what made the difference? I said, it was a

process. not any one thing made a difference, but several things combined.

now I'm ready to write to my dad. I am ready to let him know that I never want to see him again. never. I'm ready to tell him how that past has affected me in my adult life.

I'm pretty sure he never went back after I was seven. after my mom died he said, crying, that he did some terrible things to me when I was young that he really regrets. I'm sure he's forgiven himself for getting out when he did.

bully for him, I say. bully for him.

may 16 / 92

the feeling that I want to hold on to right now is the feeling that I have as a result of margaret's acceptance of me, her reaching out. it will stay with me for a long time, perhaps all my life. the importance of this woman to me, my gratitude,

        is

I just wish I could put it into words.

                maybe it's not words

two people are standing over the baby arms high in the air
long shiny long knives slow slow slow motion they stab the
baby both at the same time pull on the knives

                                       I close my eyes

                                               the man
hurts me pinches my cheeks open those fucking eyes they
reach inside the baby and each pull something out they bite
on it like dogs pull pieces off and eat it eat it I'm scared
they look scary mean scary they pass them around everyone
takes bites then they pass it to the man he looks happy mean
bites it eats it circles around me mean stuffs it in my
mouth

                                          eat

                                          eat you cunt

                                          eat

                    no I won't

                          no I won't

There are many people who cannot speak of their experiences.
Too many lives have been horribly affected by ritual abuse.
Its elements of unreality only feed back into it when its victims
are dismissed as being "ill" because of what they are reporting.
Survivors may gain some optimism if others try their best to
listen and understand — as difficult as it will be. I would like to
express my appreciation to anyone who is concerned enough to
listen and believe us, because only with acknowledgement of
this violence can we take steps towards ending it.

— R. J.

I'll write the rest

he cuts the rope and puts me gently on the floor the people
come over all happy some kissing me a man comes over with a
dress like his it's small holes for arms he puts the dress
on me I can hardly stand scared numb it's my dad he's crying
he's happy I think or sad

                                    he gives me to the man the
man takes me outside across the dark to the house he pulls
me and he's mean he takes me down into the cellar rotting
potatoes oh my tummy I know if I throw up he'll make me eat
it he sits on a stool and tells me to kneel in front of him

the rest later I need to sleep right now

BECKYLANE'S SISTER: Well this is the only family I've got. Family is family. Blood is thicker than water, ya know? Poor Mom. Poor Mom. She was so young when she died. Never a day went by that she didn't do something for one of her kids, let me tell you. Ya know, I don't remember a thing before I was twelve years old, but I've never once dreamed of blaming it on poor Mom and Dad. Lots of people don't remember their childhoods. So what?

may 17 / 92
very difficult but empowering days. I've written a letter to my dad, to my siblings.
I am having my voice.
the words abuse and incest and alcoholism have never been spoken in my family. I felt so empowered after writing to my dad, but after writing to the rest of my family, I felt hollow. uncertain. not because I doubted what I said, but more because I don't have a family anymore and I'm not so sure I want to. I know I don't want that same family. for sure.

———

Slander.   The speaking of base and defamatory words tending
to prejudice another in his reputation, office, trade, business, or
means of livelihood . . . The essential elements of slander are:
(a) a false and defamatory statement concerning another;
(b) an unprivileged communication; (c) fault amounting at least
to negligence on the part of the publisher; and (d) either
actionability of the statement irrespective of harm or the
existence of special harm. Restatement, Second, Torts § 558.

— Black's Law Dictionary, 5th Edition

may 19 / 92
still.
fast difficult empowering tiring.

I kneel in front of him he pulls me into his groin forces
his hard penis into my mouth pulls my hair my head gag I
faint he beats me beats me

                                        awake I vomit faint again he beats
me kicks me awake awake he pushes my head into the cement into my
vomit eat cunt

                                I close my eyes eat it's red all red
close my eyes don't taste so tired so weak
                                                he throws the baby
down onto the cement laughs loud scary screams kicks me no I want to
die
                he picks the baby up
                                        throws her down again the
sound the sound is all around the baby hitting the floor quiet flat loud
I block my ears crouch crouch no no I want
to die

_____

may 24 / 92

such hard work. so much. feel okay so fragile I'll do this I
know I will.
today I'll mail the letters to my family. to my dad.
I want to be able to share my feelings. alone is too much.
right now, I feel grief/sadness for myself, no childhood so
much for me to deal with when I was such a little girl.
the other day samantha said to me, you know, my life has been
horrible. this is the best time of my life. I finally feel happy.
she's right. her life has been as horrible as any kid's life should
be. she's had a lot to deal with. divorce custody abuse confusion.
but mine. my childhood. no child should ever ever have to have.
and with it the residue, baked in, of self-hate of shame. social
and professional denial. so many suffering children who need to
be saved. so many. so many adult survivors who need to be heard
to be believed to be healed to be held.

may 25 / 92

and I don't have to have those feelings come flooding back at me
to relive.
    I've lived them
    I've felt them

                helpless there's something
terribly wrong with me I'm the devil's cunt
                    the physical pain
   word-destroying   the emotional agony
no. I only have to claim it all to acknowledge that, yes,

I experienced those feelings, and by some miracle, I survived it.
        what I need now is nurture
                            the nurture I've never had
                            nurture, self-nurture is not enough
                            nurture is a sharing
                here
    share this apple   cut it in half
                here
    share this pain   cut it in half
to start with clinical nurture? the past recreated in a clinical relationship. doing some of what was missed the first time around.
bonding and trusting a primary care-giver in order to bond with
and trust myself. learn to crawl and then to walk.
this is not scary horror unnatural like then when I was expected
to do what no human can

The reason so few of these cases are successfully prosecuted
is that the information is so unpleasant that no one wants to
believe it. The investigators hear these stories and they say to
themselves, "No, this can't be true," and so they don't write it
down, they don't document it. There's often a lack of physical
evidence. The prosecutors don't want to hurt their careers by
taking cases they're unlikely to prove in court. So these cases
are frequently dropped rather than dealt with.

                                        — Sandi Gallant

to fly

teach yourself to fly, damn it. you are not human.

                                        my original intention was to
                                        write out the rest of the

it's already dead ya stupid kid just tryna
loosen up them joints a bit ya know come on
ya stupid kid I'll kill ya too ya little fuck
daddy's girl eh

my daddy loves me yes he does
there is no safe place

here ya little fuck holds up a large sack I can smell it it
smells good smells rough dusty smooth comfort
open those fucking eyes
pick it up pick it up cunt

he picks her up breaks her arm her elbow here
pig break 'em up so's they'll fit

I start to shake go cold all cold all cold

no like this
grabs my arms above my wrists my hands fill
his
breaks the other arm
now the legs stupid
you'll be next ya stupid kid

BECKYLANE'S REPORT CARD, AGE 7: Beckylane is an excellent worker. She has great future possibilities. Arithmetic is Beckylane's best subject. She is very dependable and tries her best.

You will soon hear pleasant news
of a personal nature.

The truth is that *ritual abuse exists*. It is hideous and devastating.
It does not exist because some evil force is trying to gain control
of the world. It exists because violence is perpetrated against
women and children, and then passed on to the next generation.
Ritual abuse is on the extreme end of a continuum of abuse.

— Elizabeth S. Rose

The philosophy of one century is the
common sense of the next.

wants me to break her legs the same
way I am surprised at how small the
wounds are on her lower abdomen how
straight colourless for how much
they pulled out my stomach starts
to turn again I stand there stunned
holding the baby the man has
started to put potatoes rank and
sweet into the large sack it's
dusty smells good I try to make
myself smell only that

he looks up at me fuckin do it cunt
or I'll break your ugly little neck

I can hardly hear him he sounds
like he is far far away I'm not
cold anymore I'm warm in fact I
close my eyes not tight but like
I'm sleeping I try to smell the bag

he knocks me off my feet throws the
baby onto me kicks dust in my face
pulls me up onto my feet and I know
I can't bear to hear that baby thud
when she falls off me I start to
scream he beats me beats me I can't
breathe I scream and scream I can't
stop he picks up the baby he's
screaming at me face purple veins I
can't hear him anymore all I can
hear is the baby's bones cracking
her legs I close my eyes tight this
time still can't breathe still
screaming he knocks me off my feet
again I don't want to get up I
can't breathe no I want to die I
want to die I start to scream the
words out of my mouth I want to die
I want to die I want to die loud I
mean it I start to feel powerful

he is screaming at me but I can't
hear him he wants me to do
something to put the baby in the
bag I scream louder she doesn't
even look like a baby anymore he
puts her in way down in I can hear
him now he's telling me how this
works how no one will ever know see
you pack em all around fuckin pack
kid he throws potatoes at me I pick
some up he holds the sack open I
see my hands all dark with blood
and dust no I want to die

he gets furious throws the bag down
thud I can't take it no I can't
take it the baby's face looking my
head hot feels too big can't stop
screaming can't

disguised in its own activity of making or unmaking my
professional future, my body refuses to co-operate with the
rules of the rational. I am not afraid of failure. I am not
afraid of death. I am not afraid of my body. I know what it
feels like to have my body taken away what it is like to beg
someone, anyone, to take my body from me. here. take it.
it's just a body. take it. only leave me alone. just leave me
alone I want to die. I know what it's like to want to die more
than anything any other reality just please let me die so I never
have to feel this pain again. raw red-hot pain. my skin ripped
from my body.
I repressed those years because I had to. I couldn't survive with
those memories in my body. but they were in my mind the whole
time and they shadowed me, everything I did for the thirty-odd
years in between. they will shadow me for the rest of my life. I
saw and heard and felt things with my body that few people do.
I am a rare bird.

pet the big red hen warm wise

Does the child talk about a "poo man" or "poop man" and a
"bath lady" or "washing lady"?

Does the child describe small children and babies being killed, carved and eaten by ritual participants, sometimes including themselves?

Does the child describe abusers wearing robes, masks, carrying candles?

Does the child report being photographed and filmed during his/her abuse?

You may attend a party where strange
customs prevail.

he goes away comes back with my dad I can't hear
any more I'm screaming and screaming my dad pushes
me toward the stairs up and outside I feel the
ground cool on my feet he pushes me into the car I
scream and scream I can't stop all the way all the
way home far and far far far all the way

he pulls me out of the car no I want to die he pushes me

into the house it's dark dark dark my mother is there
they are talking my mother turns on the light she is
looking at me bursts into tears comes to me holds me I
start to stop to stop screaming she says my god what have
you done to her holds me too tight I can smell her smells
of clean clothes smells of cigarette smoke holds me too

tight

Does the child report being threatened with guns or knives?

Does the child report being held under water?

Does the child report saying that abusers threatened to kill their parents, siblings or pets if they told?

A DREAM: I'm standing looking at/through a glass wall into my past into that outdoor scene that leads to the ritual abuse. the glass shatters and moves through the air behind me. it looks like glass but it is not it's more a vapour. no sharp edges no danger only silver shining gone. then a wind blows out at me strong but not pushing more air current with my body same temperature. then a short calm and the current comes from behind and moves into the trees. a layer of skin of blood peels itself off me it's me it's my entire body skin raised up into the air floats. the current continues the blood-skin dancing/floating shrinking disappears away. then a mist, a grey mist, dissipates from the scene and it is bright daylight.

may 28 / 92
my past no longer coming at me me coming at my past.

A SCHOLAR: You describe your past like a newspaper reporter
and what's in the news is horrific.

jun 05 / 92
have you ever noticed that your family, your dad your brothers
and sisters, treat you like you're invisible? wayne asked me three
or four years ago. them all there and no one heard wayne.
I hadn't noticed before then. I loved wayne, felt such love for
him at that moment.

Some examples are torture with pins and needles, forcing a child
to take mind-altering drugs, and submerging a child in water,
particularly as part of a satanic baptismal ritual. Other tactics include withholding of food or water, sleep deprivation, and forced
eating of feces, urine, blood, or raw flesh.

— Elizabeth S. Rose

elie weisel survived the nazi holocaust. he says, rejected
by [human]kind, the condemned do not go so far as to reject
it in return. their faith in history remains unshaken,
and one can well wonder why. they do not despair.
the proof: they persist in surviving — not
only to survive, but to testify. the
victims elect to become witnesses.

I am a stick   stiff
I stop crying but I can't talk
no I can't
she takes me upstairs so gentle soothing
crying bathes me rubs too hard
        my dad skulks in the doorway my mom says
            don't you ever take her there again
                looks at me rubs too hard

you're nothing but trouble I knew it the day you were
                            born   nothing but
                                    trouble
she puts me to bed but not in my bed
        in the basement on a cot
I can smell the clean sheets
        my clean pyjamas

———

after that I couldn't talk
I got sick don't remember much
the doctor came finally and my parents took me out of
the special program at school
the doctor said it must be too hard on me my mom promised I
could go to my aunty's this summer if I started to talk I
could hear and I could understand but I couldn't talk they
said

faker
faker
nothin but a faker
my brothers and sisters

then one day I got up and went into
the front porch closed the door I had
brought my stool stood on it to look at
myself in the mirror stare hate stare hate hate
for me I hate you I hate you I hate you I hate you
strong long

look
look at me look at me
hate I hate you
hate hate look at me look
at me
hate break the mirror bleeding
bleeding no I want to die

One day I was able to get up, after gathering all my strength. I
wanted to see myself in the mirror hanging on the opposite wall.
I had not seen myself since the ghetto.
From the depths of the mirror, a corpse gazed back at me.
The look in his eyes, as they stared into mine, has never left me.
— Elie Wiesel

jun 07 / 92
full circle. that's the day I tried to kill myself. the day
my mirror image became other.
I'm exhausted. beat.
success.

Leave your boat and travel
on firm ground.

jun 08 / 92

I wept yesterday last night this morning now. everything
all mixed up in whether or not I deserve to be loved to love
myself then from now with all my healing nurturing maturity.
soothing love.
I weep because my parents didn't love me. I longed for their
love held onto any small
I weep because my little body was stolen from me by my parents
by my uncle by my dad's friends by strangers. so much physical
pain so much so that I barely experienced moments without
physical pain. beatings. twisting bones where they don't twist.
eating pee and vomit and faeces and semen blood guts maggots
until food seemed tasteless I taught myself not to taste not to feel
texture temperature. beaten into senselessness hit in the back of
the head, left side, left side, left side so often that now when I lie
on the right, disoriented eyes can't find their centre so dizzy so
much movement in my head hold it doesn't help just try to roll
the hell off the right side of my head.
I weep now because, then, I learned to believe I deserved that
treatment. I was not a normal child. I was the devil's cunt.
I weep because the gap is so wide. the gap between my desire
for self-love and my ability to love myself.
water myself with love. allergic to my own tears. to my own
sweat my body's water.
I weep because the pain is so incredible too much to keep to
myself yet the pain of sharing seems unbearable.
the pain of sharing. should be the heal of sharing.

jun 12 / 92

I've come through slaughter. I've watched animals children babies slaughtered. in through my eyes. into my body. I wasn't slaughtered but I've had my body tortured into numbness. into never wanting to hurt another living creature.

jun 14 / 92

am I going to give up? put it on the shelf? the shelves are almost empty. all the books removed and only years of dust to wipe away after I finish this one last book. then put all the books back and pull one or another off to reread from time to time. that's where I want to be. to begin again.

And remember, the best revenge is writing well.

— Audrey Thomas

10 Reasons Why I Would Falsely Accuse My Parents of Incest or Ritual Abuse

4. I needed a new reason to stay in therapy.
8. I wanted to be different, special and get lots of attention by breaking down and becoming incapable of supporting or taking care of myself.

— Jezanna Rainforest

fetal sit.
do you weep when you are alone?
do you heal when you are alone?
to manifest grief or other strong emotion by
shedding tears; to mourn, lament.
fetal sit.

A SCHOLAR: The interweaving of quotations from other accounts of abuse survival, diary entries, images welling up from repressed memories, fortune cookie proclamations, etc. is very effective. With the exception of a bit of excessive repetition of the heroics of survival near the end

jun 18 / 92

I was so brave. so incredibly brave I wish I could do more for me
could time-travel, physically. go back, me now, and help me when
I was so small. hold me. not too tight. say, oh my little darling, I
love you so. you are safe now. come here sit here with me and I'll
hold you I'll keep you safe you are safe you will be safe forever.
no one will ever hurt you again. no one. you can laugh and play
and sing. no one will tell you you are bad. no one will tell you
you are evil, because you aren't. you are just a little girl. see?
I'm big and you are small. you're a precious little girl and no
one should hurt you. no one should tell you you are bad. you
are good you are good rock me sing me hold me hum
                                        smooth line hum
                                                        quiet
rocking until my little body stops shaking stops being
afraid feels safe. still safe. safe today and today and
today until it's tomorrow and still safe.

fill my days with silence. wind water wet soil smells of
here birds everywhere making dance and music and life.
everybody's alone no one is alone. this longing.
the gap can't be filled, beckylane.
but it can be healed.
there is no mean and evil side to me there never was. I thought
there must be but I just couldn't see it. my eyes are open now.
wide I can see now. I deserve the best from me. I'm getting there.
day by day. believing in myself.
this has been a long process. it will take longer. I'll get there
to where I feel safe.

I had to take my time, take a month to write out this most recent memory. after I read it out loud to myself the first time, I close my eyes and ask myself, what do I see? I see a hill with grass blown into the hill. a tumbleweed rolls with the wind. something which seems dead but is preparing to root itself, to find a new place to germinate. it is beautiful in its own way and in its own way, soft. fragile but durable. it has thorns which injure people. not intended for people at all, but to cause it to catch and root.

                    me a messenger gaping holes wind blows through
                              from the past

B etween the ages of eleven and thirty-three, I abandoned my feet and I spent my adolescence and most of my adult life flying. I felt like I was flying through the night so my dreams wouldn't catch up with me, like I was flying inside clouds and shadows during the day so no one would see me. My energy level was high, but my movements were slow: I was a slow eater, a slow walker, slow to talk, slow to anger. Now I'm like a land-bird, big and rebirthed red and soft and warm. I'm in my early forties and my movements are still slow. I like that about myself now. It gives me lots of time to heal.

I would now say that in many ways my healing really began only after I recovered the one memory charted in this book. At that time, my therapist was my major source of support. It was close to impossible for me to speak about my past, even to her. My seemingly endless focus on "loving myself" during this period was literally the only way I could keep myself alive. I can't overstress just how intensive ritual abuse programming is. It's designed to work. In this sense, I think a reader who is also a survivor of abuse may not experience this repetition as tedium or as an apolitical stance. Ritual abuse is misogyny that's rolled right off the edge of the globe and the extent of violence against women and children is the pull that keeps it there. Ritual abuse is still very well hidden. Power and protection are available to the perpetrators, and the survivors are kept silent. I know of at least four women and men who are ritual abuse survivors who were abused in the same city. They've approached the police and the Crown and have provided (without knowing about each other) names of perpetrators where several of the names correspond. One of these names is of a prominent politician. The Crown refuses to prosecute (even for incest) any of the people whose names are on the list, including the survivors' fathers and/or mothers.

These survivors were acting out of positions of empowerment and hope when they approached the police. All of them had been in long-term counselling and laying charges was part of their healing process. Because counsellors are still involving themselves in the "believe-it-or-not debate," or have worked in isolation from one another, they continue to encourage clients to press charges of ritual abuse, and these charges are followed by long-term bureaucratic legal brick walls. There are multi-generational ritual abuse groups which practice from various positions of sophistication and which operate on a worldwide networking basis. The group I was forced into, like the ones described by these other women and men, was multi-generational.

Violence is definitely politically/ideologically/systemically formed and informed, but when you're remembering and recording graphic details of severe abuse that was done to you during infancy and early childhood, when your world comes undone and the years and months give up their hold, when your kids/your friends/your writing/your jobs/your reading can't keep you in the present, you know it's *you* who has to change. Coming to know this helped me tremendously toward healing. A survivor of ritual abuse has the added burden of deprogramming. You learn to *know* that you're hateful. Loving myself was absolutely the most difficult task I took on during my counselling. And it certainly wasn't my counsellor's idea. It's something I was unable to share even with her.

I began counselling after I lost a custody dispute with my former husband. I became seriously depressed so I began to see a feminist counsellor. Several months later, when issues around the custody were less debilitating, I asked my counsellor if we could work on some other issues.

The day of my mother's death, a few years earlier, was the day I started to have memories of my childhood. Until then, I had had only two memories and both of these were from before I was two years old. My childhood from age two to eleven was a blank. When I started to remember my childhood in my early thirties, there was a one-year period, between ages six and seven, of which I had no memories. The other years began slowly to fill themselves in. I had had memories of serious abuse. I wanted to talk about that and I wanted to try hypnotherapy to see if I could remember that one year. I had done some desensitization work with this counsellor around my fear of my former husband and it had been very successful. I used hypnosis off and on throughout my counselling, though most of my memories returned outside therapy. I found regressive hypnosis to be far too immediate — it's a "returning to" the event. It's not even "like" being there again; it's *being* there again.

By the end of my first year of therapy I was remembering more of my parents' abuse toward me and I was beginning to remember my father involving me in abuse at farms away from home.

My therapist didn't put words like "ritual abuse" to some of my memories, and neither did I until well into my second year of counselling when I attended a conference where the focus was violence against women. During her keynote presentation, a ritual abuse survivor showed slides of women's visual expressions of their experiences of ritual abuse. I felt as if I'd seen that before, it was all so familiar. But I denied that to myself at the time. I reacted so strongly, though. I became cold to my bones and barely able to walk, unable to talk. Soon after the conference, I began to remember parts of the year between the ages of six and seven. I then spent almost a full year working to recover that lost time, and the diary entries in this book are part of the memory work done during that year of recall.

Time and continued healing have distanced me somewhat from my three years in therapy, and I would now say I don't think individual counselling for ritual abuse survivors is the best idea. I think it puts too much responsibility on both the counsellor and the client. One of the messages I internalized during torture was *don't trust anyone*, especially those in positions of power and those in the social science professions. Consequently, I didn't feel enough trust with my counsellor to speak freely, and this was a problem throughout my three years of therapy. At different times I wanted to talk about power in our client-counsellor relationship but my counsellor felt that that wouldn't be constructive. I wanted to know more about her as a person and she felt that that would be artificial, that this was my counselling. Even so, I would say that I learned many skills in counselling which still work to help me to continue to heal, such as self-directed healing, listening to my body and my spirit, deep muscle relaxation, and compartmentalizing. I went into counselling with many strengths already:

political awareness, research skills, critical reading, diary writing, creative writing, patience, hope, a sense of humour, and deep compassion. All of these have contributed to my healing.

I haven't had the opportunity to be involved in group work, so I can't comment on that. And I waver on that one too. I've often thought about how liberating it would be just to be able to share experiences with other women who've gone through ritual abuse. But then I think about how key the facilitator would be to that process and how difficult the facilitator's job would be. It was extremely difficult for me to keep up with my responsibilities as mother/friend/student/teacher/client when I was in counselling and remembering ritual abuse. I disagree, however, with the notion of what I consider self-absorbed, narcissistic healing strategies — where everyone around the survivor (including partner, children, etc.) is meant to put their lives on hold for three to five years while the survivor locks herself in her bedroom or "takes care of [only] herself," and no matter how she decides to go about doing that, it's just okay, because it works for her.

I guess I feel I needed some method of counselling that doesn't exist right now. I believe work done with ritual abuse survivors would best be done with a non-hierarchical team of workers, and not just PH.D'd or university-educated workers, but maybe some high-functioning recovering survivors, spiritual healers, and healing members of communities. It's important to heal in body, mind, heart, and spirit. In order to accomplish any one of these, I believe it would take a lot more than a one-on-one counsellor-client coming-from-Freud-whether-we-acknowledge-it-or-not relationship.

In Native cultures, for example, healing is understood as a

community responsibility. I know of teamwork being done with survivors (and their families) of extreme and horrific abuse in residential schools. The work is intense and difficult, but a team of healers works with the survivors on healing body, mind, heart, and spirit, and the survivors don't go off to work or classes or home at the end of the day. The setting doesn't look, feel, smell, or taste like a hospital, a counsellor's office, or an institution for the sick. I personally would like to see something similar available for ritual abuse survivors.

I don't think it's my place to provide answers or to suggest that I know what might help other women through their healing process, though I can say what's been helpful for me. I would say I survived my childhood by letting my body mind go to sleep, and with my spirit mind I moved out of my body. I spent inordinate amounts of time by myself and in the nearby river valley while I was growing up. I wasn't alone there, but of course white middle-class psychology doesn't know or acknowledge the healing powers of all our relations.

In order to survive my childhood, I created two children, one inside and one outside myself. I created Lane when I was four or five, and she was my way of holding on to my "inside me" throughout my childhood. Lane was with me until my dad killed my dog when I was eleven, and then she went into the river to live with the rocks and took my childhood memories with her. During my first session of hypnosis, I chose the river valley where I grew up as my safe place. I went straight down the steep hill and to the rapids and Lane came straight out from the waterfoam. I created Becky when I was seven years old. Becky was my way of putting my ritual abuse experiences and my self-hatred to rest "outside" myself and inside a mirror. (I subsequently smashed the mirror and tried to kill myself/my image with the broken glass. This enabled me to speak after months of being unable to do so.) With tender love and self-gratitude, I've (re)called these parts of myself "Beckylane," my pseudonym for this book. Recovering the parts of myself where I stored my childhood memories was the most helpful part of my healing process.

I'm not what I would call a multiple personality "reorder." I think the concept of multiple personality disorder or MPD is overrated and keeps university-educated healers from seeking out or even acknowledging the spectrum of survivor skills. Some of the skills I used as a kid sound very similar to those used by multiples, but I seem to have also used other ways of surviving the torture and other ways of coping with my own involvement. I would make myself into a bug, for example, when I was being deprived of food and water. Bugs don't eat much. Bugs don't drink much. I would make myself into a crow when I had to be loud and aggressive. I made myself into different trees for their strength and spirit, into plants, leaves, veins of leaves, into flowers, animals, water, odours, light. I can literally slow time down and experience things in slow motion, either when I'm there in a situation, or later when I'm remembering it.

I can't begin to say how valuable hearing and reading about other people's survival skills was and is to me in my healing work. There are checklists for social scientists (and for clients) to help them to determine whether or not a person may have suffered from abuse as a child. But, incredibly, there are no checklists which detail the astounding and inspiring skills children create in order to survive their abuse. It helped me so much to read or to hear or to know that what I thought of as a daft or bizarre behaviour was actually used by other children too. Children are close to their behaviours because they're in them. They're not too self-conscious, so they tell it like it is, explaining why they do what they do. Children's stories bring hope with them: their self-nurturing abilities and their continued willingness to trust those adults who offer care take my breath away.

Social scientists know about survivors' skills because their clients have taught these to them. I believe it's important to keep this in mind and to demystify and humanize the counsellor-client relationship, to depathologize the language so that survivors don't continue to get the message that they're sick and inadequately equipped to heal themselves. As for those millions of people (yes, they really do exist) who can't afford counselling services but who can read, where are their experiences articulated? And for those who do not or cannot read? For those who can't hear?

Survivors of abuse are not sick. The extent of systemic violence is. Systemic violence is created and practised by people. Why do people continually rationalize violence, especially against women and children? Why do people fail to recognize their own violent behaviours? Why is oppression not named as violence? I don't have answers to these questions and I'm hoping that making my story public will encourage people to feel more compassion and to understand family violence and incest and ritual abuse for the serious spiritual ailments that they are.

Going public with my experiences has helped me continue my healing. I'm not suggesting that this would be helpful to everyone, but I'm a writer and writing is part of how I feel I can heal myself and speak to other abuse survivors. My focus throughout this book was on my own struggle toward healing and acceptance, and on public education about the heinous reality of ritual abuse. My goal was to present explicit details and at the same time to deny a voyeuristic reading. Details of abuse may be a turn-on to some readers, yet at the same time may cut through the intense denial around abuse. I endeavoured to concretize and foreground the effects of abuse on childhood development by concentrating on the inadequacy of language and the ways in which pain and torture destroy one's ability to speak.

I've read a tremendous number of books written by survivors of incest and abuse and this reading was most helpful when I was unable to share my healing process with others or when I was having trouble understanding my own behaviours. Moreover, this reading helped me rebuild my ability to speak about my childhood. I became keenly aware of the courage involved in publishing abuse narratives in the present climate of potential lawsuits and public denial. Yet I noticed, too, that there's a huge gaping hole where the work and words of women who come from unprivileged backgrounds should be — women who shared their bedrooms with three or four or more siblings, whose experiences might best speak to me and millions of other women. Middle-class women can afford counselling, can afford schooling, can queen's english their personal accounts off to publishers.

I would like to see the focus shift from social science professionals being seen as the experts on incest and ritual abuse, to the survivors themselves being recognized as the experts. Child abuse isn't theory. Like racism, it's lived, it's personal, it's immediate, it's emotional. It hurts. As a political act, I've begun to speak publicly about ritual abuse and my experience has been that people can't hear even a fraction of what happened to me. They're curious, so they ask direct questions about ritual abuse and about what happened to me. Then their eyes glaze over. They leave the room. They change the subject. They blame me for the severity of the abuse. They want me to soften the impact for them. They want me to take care of them. I don't see these reactions as healthy. I get tired of being expected to take responsibility for ritual abuse. I get tired of being left alone in a room after a group of people suddenly have something pressing to do when they can't hear the answers to their own questions. I get tired of being moved to tears (I'm able to cry now) when I'm responding, and then the people step back and pull their hands into themselves, like they're doing a dance.

I know how "lucky" I am to have gotten out when I was seven. There isn't language in my heart that's strong enough to describe what *would've* happened to me when I got older if I'd still been involved in ritual abuse activities. I wasn't old enough to be a "breeder," where my own father and other men would rape me, beat me, torture me, impregnate me, and then hand me over to the resident physicians who would deliver my babies, only to murder them right in front of me or force me to murder my own children. I was old enough to be prostituted out to other ritual abuse groups (and I was), but my teen years were mine. I won't say I'm thankful for that because soft, fluffy words like that don't fit with the anger that wells up inside me when I think of the thousands of twelve- and thirteen-year-old girls who still have years of terror to face while the public toys with terms like "false memory syndrome," says things like "fascinating" and "well, there'd be birth certificates, there'd be death certificates," and "No, this can't be happening. Who'd *do* things like that to children? Surely we'd know. There'd be evidence. They can't be so clever that they'd outsmart us all."

Words are so important. They communicate what's in people's hearts. Right now, people reward ritual abuse perpetrators through language. People condone ritual abuse through language. Words like "clever" and "outsmart" have positive connotations and are valued by the public. People say, "We can't take these guys to court, they're influential leaders of our society." In reality, they're cannibals who pass as upstanding citizens during working hours. For play, they'd rape and dismember your little girls and then make you watch while they eat them. This isn't a matter for belief or disbelief. Stop using language that discredits the survivors and praises the slaughterers. There's no time for that kind of word-play. Survivors who are taken seriously and given the respect and admiration they deserve can work with the "experts" to find ways to infiltrate and stop ritual abuse networks.

I'm aware that perpetrators may try to discredit me and will look for inconsistencies in order to undermine the book's credibility. A good place for police to begin their investigations would be behind the closed doors of those who discredit ritual abuse, and then of those who promote False Memory Syndrome. Syndrome is a medical term that's misused in this psychological context. It's a media term they say was coined (anonymously) by a white, upper-middle-class professional and alleged paedophile, and it's a concept that is supported by people who condone brutal beatings and rapes of children and women. I have a friend whose mother helped children to shelter during the second world war. One afternoon after a massive bombing, she and her sister went out into the streets to find children who had survived. There were mangled and dismembered children everywhere. The woman doesn't remember this part of the afternoon. She remembers going out into the streets and she remembers being with the children inside the shelter. Her sister remembers the details in between. Does this mean that when and if this woman recovers her memory of that afternoon, her memory will be "false"?

I'm aware that ritual abuse perpetrators may try to identify me and possibly even harass me. And no, I don't feel safe in this regard. But there are tens of thousands of children and women who don't have the luxury of feeling either safe or unsafe. It's to them that I dedicate this book, to all the infants and toddlers, children and adolescents, women and men, who've suffered and/or died and who still suffer and/or die at the hands of these slaughterers.

During the years since my individual counselling, I've remembered more and more detail of the rituals, and more recently, details of the torture I was subjected to. And I don't know what made the ritual abuse stop when I was seven. Maybe my mother's intervention. Maybe something else, but my father didn't take me back after I attempted suicide following months of sickness and silence. The time of packing the dead baby was the last time my father took me there. I was still faced with severe abuse at home from both my parents and some of my siblings. I was quiet, non-violent, and I excelled in school.

I think it's important for me to emphasize that my childhood used to weigh much more heavily on my self-perception than it does now that I've worked long and hard to separate the actual abuse that was done *to* my person from me as a person. My marriage partner was also abusive, so my progress was slow. A few years into my personal healing work, I realized that I was trying to change my inside behaviour while remaining in an environment that fostered and "nurtured," if you will, an extreme sense of worthlessness. I was a receptacle for abuse. I was threatened with physical violence (household objects, walls, doors, floors, food), raped, and utterly debased verbally. These abuses were a part of my day-to-day life. My husband loved me, that much seemed clear. He indicated that in many other ways. Because this violence was sweet relief after the violence I'd been raised with, it was years before I was able to think past that and to name the violence that did exist in my marriage. After a couple of years of marriage counselling and increased violence, I ended my marriage. I also severed ties with my family of origin several years ago. There was just nothing that was positive for me there. These were difficult and necessary steps in my healing.

Abused children are given the message that theirs is an isolated reality. At the same time, the message they get from video games, television, movies, churches, schools, and play is that violence is a game (mostly) men get rewarded for. And that's how my family worked. I rewarded my husband's and my parents' violent behaviours with good food, clean house, quiet as a mouse. I have rewarded my own kids differently. I've taught them the kinds of creative, healing ways I learned from the plants and animals and water I became intimate with as a child and with whom I maintain my intimacy.

Because I'm not protected against lawsuits as a survivor of ritual abuse, I can't use my birth name. I can't properly thank my aunty Sahara, who gave me (and still does) the love and comfort my parents couldn't, because Sahara's not her birth name either.

It's the name she chose for herself here, though, and she chose it because she says when she blows, you know it. I say, thanks for blowin your wind my way, Aunty. And thanks to all the rest of you who've given yourselves names in my book. Because of all of you, my healing continues. My kids, Samantha and Gregory. My "family of choice," Sally, Arel, Aladin, and Monique. My good friends Wilhelmina, Anjali, Mary-Jane, Jesse, Wayne, and Jim. My prof Stephanie, my counsellor, Margaret, and the many others who haven't named themselves for this book. We know who you are. Thanks for the memories.

SELECTED BIBLIOGRAPHY

Amethya. "Amethya's Story." *Herizons* 6, no. 3 (1992): 19–23.

Annette. "They Couldn't Get My Soul." In *The Courage to Heal: A Guide for Women Survivors of Child Sexual Abuse*, edited by Ellen Bass and Laura Davis. New York: Harper & Row, 1988.

Black, Henry Campbell, et al. *Black's Law Dictionary: Definitions of the Terms and Phrases of American and English Jurisprudence, Ancient and Modern*. 5th ed. St. Paul, Minn.: West Publishing Company, 1979.

Boyd, Andrew. *Blasphemous Rumours: Is Satanic Ritual Abuse Fact or Fantasy? An Investigation*. Glasgow: HarperCollins Manufacturing, 1991.

Cassens-Moss, Debra. "Are the Children Lying?" *ABA Journal* (1987): 59–62.

Cook, Caren. "Understanding Ritual Abuse: Through a Study of Thirty-Three Ritual Abuse Survivors from Thirteen Different States." Undergraduate Honors Thesis, University of Colorado at Boulder, 1991.

Courtois, C. A. "The Memory Retrieval Process in Incest Survivor Therapy." *Journal of Child Sexual Abuse* 1, no. 1 (1992): 15–31.

Cozolino, Louis J. "The Ritual Abuse of Children: Implications for Clinical Practice and Research." *Journal of Sex Research* 26, no. 1 (1989): 131–38.

Dan. "Dan's Story." In *Breaking the Circle of Satanic Ritual Abuse: Recognizing and Recovering from the Hidden Trauma*, by Daniel Ryder. Minneapolis: CompCare Publishers, 1992.

Danica, Elly. *Don't: A Woman's Word*. Charlottetown: Gynergy Books, 1988.

Edwards, Louise M. "Differentiating Between Ritual Assault and Sexual Abuse." In *In the Shadow of Satan: The Ritual Abuse of Children*. Special Issue of *Journal of Child and Youth Care* (1990): 67–90.

Fisher-Taylor, Gail. "Ritual Abuse: Towards a Feminist Understanding." *Herizons* 6, no. 3 (1992): 19–23.

Fraser, Sylvia. *My Father's House: A Memoir of Incest and of Healing*. Toronto: Collins Paperback, 1988 (c1987).

Gallant, Sandi. "Sandi Gallant: Ritual-Abuse Investigator." In *The Courage to Heal: A Guide for Women Survivors of Child Sexual Abuse*, edited by Ellen

Bass and Laura Davis, 417–21. New York: Harper & Row, 1988.

Gould, Catherine. "Diagnosis and Treatment of Ritually Abused Children." In *Out of Darkness: Exploring Satanism and Ritual Abuse,* edited by David K. Sakheim and Susan E. Devine, 207–48. Don Mills: Maxwell Macmillan Canada, 1992.

Hudson, Pamela S. [a] "Ritual Child Abuse: A Survey of Symptoms and Allegations." In *In the Shadow of Satan: The Ritual Abuse of Children.* Special Issue of *Journal of Child and Youth Care* (1990): 27–54.

Hudson, Pamela S. [b] *Ritual Child Abuse: Discovery, Diagnosis and Treatment.* Saratoga, Cal.: R&E Publishers, 1991.

Kahaner, Larry. *Cults That Kill.* New York: Warner Books, 1988.

Katchen, Martin H. "The History of Satanic Religions." In *Out of Darkness: Exploring Satanism and Ritual Abuse,* edited by David K. Sakheim and Susan E. Devine, 1–19. Don Mills: Maxwell Macmillan Canada, 1992.

Kelly, Susan J. "Parental Stress Response to Sexual Abuse and Ritualistic Abuse of Children in Day-Care Centres." *Nursing Research* 39, no. 1 (1990): 25–29.

Kent, Cheryl Carey. "Ritual Abuse." In *Case Studies in Family Violence,* edited by Robert T. Ammerman and Michel Hersen, 187–207. New York: Plenum Press, 1991.

Lanning, Kenneth V. "A Law-Enforcement Perspective on Allegations of Ritual Abuse." In *Out of Darkness: Exploring Satanism and Ritual Abuse,* edited by David K. Sakheim and Susan E. Devine, 109–46. Don Mills: Maxwell Macmillan Canada, 1992.

Makin, Kirk. [a] "If There's a Gap the Mind Fills It." *The Globe and Mail,* 3 July 1993: A5.

Makin, Kirk. [b] "Memories of Abuse: Real or Imagined?" *The Globe and Mail,* 3 July 1993: A1.

Maracle, Lee. *I Am Woman.* North Vancouver: Write-on Press Publishers, 1988.

Marron, Kevin. *Ritual Abuse.* Toronto: Seal Books, 1988.

Mayer, Robert S. *Satan's Children: Case Studies in Multiple Personality.* New York: G. P. Putnam's Sons, 1991.

Nurcombe, Barry, and Jurgen Unutzer. "The Ritual Abuse of Children: Clinical Features and Diagnostic Reasoning." *Journal of the American Academy of Child and Adolescent Psychiatry* 30, no. 2 (1991): 272–76.

Peters, James. "Ritual Abuse? Facts, Fallacies and Hidden Agendas." Paper presented at symposium, Ritual Abuse: Fact or Fiction? The Institute for the Prevention of Child Abuse Convention, Alymer, Ontario, 29 May 1989.

Potvin, Elizabeth Ann. *White Lies (For My Mother)*. Edmonton: NeWest Publishers, 1992.

Putnam, Frank W. "The Satanic Ritual Abuse Controversy." *Child Abuse and Neglect* 15, no. 3 (1991): 175–79.

R.J. "R.J.'s Story." *Herizons* 6, no. 3 (1992): 19–23.

Rainforest, Jezanna. "10 Reasons Why I Would Falsely Accuse My Parents of Incest or Ritual Abuse." In *Body Memories* [which loosely re-created this list from a flyer by *FIST* (Fabulous Incest Survivor's Tirade)].

Raschke, Carl A. *Painted Black: From Drug Killings to Heavy Metal — The Alarming True Story of How Satanism is Terrorizing Our Communities*. San Francisco: Harper & Row, 1990.

Ritual Abuse Task Force, Los Angeles County Commission for Women. *Ritual Abuse: Definition, Glossary, and the Use of Mind Control*. Los Angeles, Cal.: Author, 15 September 1989.

Rose, Elizabeth S. "Surviving the Unbelievable: Cult Ritual Abuse." *Ms.*, III, 4 (1993): 40–45.

Ryder, Daniel. *Breaking the Circle of Satanic Ritual Abuse: Recognizing and Recovering from the Hidden Trauma*. Minneapolis: CompCare Publishers, 1992.

Sakheim, David K., and Susan E. Devine, eds. *Out of Darkness: Exploring Satanism and Ritual Abuse*. Don Mills: Maxwell Macmillan Canada, 1992.

Scarry, Elaine. *The Body in Pain: The Making and Unmaking of the World*. New York: Oxford University Press, 1985.

Sleeth, Pamela, and Jan Barnsley. *Recollecting Our Lives: Women's Experience of Childhood Sexual Abuse*. Vancouver: Press Gang Publishers, 1989.

Smith, Margaret. *Ritual Abuse: What It Is, Why It Happens, and How To Help*. San Franscisco: HarperSanFranscisco, 1993.

Smith, Michelle, and Lawrence Pazder. *Michelle Remembers*. New York: Congdon and Lattes Press, 1980.

Sorensen, Teena, and Barbara Snow. "How Children Tell: The Process of Disclosure in Child Sexual Abuse." *Child Welfare* 70, no. 1 (1991): 3–15.

Spencer, Judith. *Suffer the Child*. New York: Simon & Schuster, 1989.

Steed, Judy. *Our Little Secret: Confronting Child Sexual Abuse in Canada*.

Toronto: Random House of Canada, 1994.

Stone, Linda, and David Stone. "Ritual Abuse: The Experiences of Five Families." In *Out of Darkness: Exploring Satanism and Ritual Abuse,* edited by David K. Sakheim and Susan E. Devine, 175–83. Don Mills: Maxwell Macmillan Canada, 1992.

Tate, Tim. *Children For the Devil: Ritual Abuse and Satanic Crime.* London: Methuen, 1991.

Thomas, Audrey. *Latakia.* Vancouver: Talonbooks, 1979.

Turcotte, Shirley. [a] "Learning to Accept What Seems Unbelievable." Paper presented at symposium, Women and Mental Health: Women in a Violent Society. Canadian Mental Health Association Convention, Banff, Alberta, 11 May 1991.

Turcotte, Shirley. [b] Paper presented at conference, Making Up for Lost Time. Stone Angel conference, Thunder Bay, Ontario, 2 November 1994.

Wakefield, Hollida, and Ralph Underwager. "Uncovering Memories of Alleged Sexual Abuse: The Therapists Who Do It." *Issues in Child Abuse Accusations* 4, no. 4 (1992): 197–213.

Warnke, Michael. *The Satan Seller.* Plainfield, N.J.: Logos International, 1972.

Webb, Phyllis. "Poetics Against the Angel of Death." In her *The Vision Tree: Selected Poems,* edited by Sharon Thesen. Vancouver: Talonbooks, 1982.

Wiesel, Elie. *Night.* Translated by Stella Rodway. 1958. Reprint. Toronto: Bantam Books, 1982.

Williams, Patricia J. *The Alchemy of Race and Rights: Diary of a Law Professor.* Cambridge: Harvard University Press, 1991.

Williamson, Janice. " 'I Peel Myself out of My Own Skin': Reading *Don't: A Woman's Word.*" In *Essays on Life Writing: From Genre to Critical Practice,* edited by Marlene Kadar, 135–51. Toronto: University of Toronto Press, 1992.

Wisechild, Louise M., ed. *She Who Was Lost is Remembered: Healing from Incest Through Creativity.* Seattle: The Seal Press, 1991.

*Press Gang Publishers Feminist Co-operative is committed to producing
quality books with social and literary merit. We give priority to
Canadian women's work and include writing by lesbians and by
women from diverse cultural and class backgrounds.
Our list features vital and provocative fiction,
poetry, and non-fiction.*

*A free catalogue is available from Press Gang Publishers,
101 - 225 East 17th Avenue, Vancouver, B.C.
V5V 1A6 Canada*